To Bob
from
Bettie Christmas 1977

Alexandria

Between Alexandria and Washington at Eighth and M southeast, this ferry operated from 1868 until it was burned in 1892.

Courtesy of Frederick Tilp

Waterfront looking north. Taken from the Pioneer Mills, 1853.

Photo by Matthew Brady
Courtesy of Frederick Tilp

Alexandria

A Pictorial History

By Karen G. Harvey and Ross Stansfield

Donning Co./Publishers
Norfolk, Virginia

The Round House was a familiar sight on Duke and Henry Streets from the mid-1800s until destroyed by arson on August 22, 1971. Originally owned by the Alexandria and Orange Railroad, it serviced locomotives until its later years when it became a storehouse for lumber.

Courtesy of Southern Railway System

Library of Congress Cataloging in Publication Data:

Harvey, Karen G 1944—
Alexandria: a pictorial history.
1. Alexandria, Va.—History—Pictorial works.
I. Stansfield, Ross, 1950— joint author.
F234.A3H37 975.5'296 77-23342
ISBN 0-915442-32-9

Printed in the United States of America

To four people whose cooperation
and support
made this book possible

John, Elinor,
George and Anna

300 block of Cameron Street circa 1900.

Courtesy of Wilson Design

ACKNOWLEDGMENTS

I wish to express my gratitude to all those who gave assistance and support in this endeavor. Of utmost importance are Mr. and Mrs. George Stansfield, parents of my associate and talented photographer, Ross. Individually and jointly Anna and George Stansfield have given immeasurable aid and advice. As a fourth generation Alexandrian, Anna has been a treasure-trove of information and rare photographs.

A special thanks also goes to Nettie Allen Voges, who shared with me a valuable possession, her understanding and love of the people of Alexandria; and to Jean Elliot, whose literary and historic guidance added substance and clarity to the text of this book.

My appreciation goes to the following, who not only contributed from private collections but gave willingly of their time and knowledge: Charles Sampson, Margery and Laurence Fawcett, Frederick Tilp, Mrs. Thomas A. (Polly) Hulfish, Helen Day, Ellen and Stanley King, and Robert Whitton.

For furnishing resource material as well as pictures, I extend my thanks to Barbara Crews, the Alexandria Tourist Council; Edward Russell, the Corps of Engineer Museum, Fort Belvoir, Virginia; Marci Larson, Southern Railways System; the ladies of the Alexandria Library; and the Alexandria Department of Planning and Community Development.

Although I will not list the names, I thank all those who helped with family histories. Hopefully something of the character and personality of these people will be expressed through the photographs and narratives of their ancestors as portrayed here.

It is impossible to thank everyone who has contributed to this venture, however I wish to gratefully acknowledge several who have given of their special talents. They are: Elsa Rosenthal, Mrs. Hugh B. Cox, Major Russell Hawes, Ray Gallagher, Doctor Mark Howard, the Reverend Chris Hobgood, Loretta Haas, and most especially my mother, Elinor Giddens Davis, and my wonderfully understanding husband, John.

Ross and I both hope that the photographs contained within this volume have captured something of the spirit of this historic town. Although all information has been carefully researched, this book is in no way intended to be a reference source; rather it is a means of conveying through pictures and words the soul of a fascinating city. We welcome all those unfamiliar with Alexandria to become acquainted. Who knows, perhaps Alexandria natives will themselves strike up new friendships as old memories are revived through the pages of this book. We hope all will enjoy it.

Karen G. Harvey
Alexandria, Virginia

Wolfe Street looking west from Lee Street, 1929.
One of the oldest streets in the United States.

Courtesy of National Archives

CONTENTS

FOREWORD

Motorists driving south on the George Washington Parkway are confronted at the city line by an overhead sign proclaiming: **Alexandria—Most Historic Community In The Nation.** This is misleading, for how can a relatively late town, founded in 1749 by act of legislature, compare for sheer weight of history to such earlier places as Salem, Massachusetts, or St. Augustine, Florida?

What the Virginia city can boast of is *concentrated* history: in the two hundred and forty-seven years since the auction of lots on July 13, 1749, this riverport has been twice enemy-occupied: by British naval forces in September 1814 and by Union troops in April 1861. Destructive conflagrations and other calamities have ravaged it.

Alexandria's relatively late birth had advantages since nothing was haphazard; nothing, unlike Topsy, "just growed"; no log cabins on those first lots. Streets, from the first, were laid out parallel, not helter-skelter, in what has now become Old Town.

There was, to be sure, a small preliminary settlement: a trading center at what today is the foot of Oronoco Street. The Scottish factors, who developed this, called it Belhaven in honor of John Hamilton (Lord Belhaven) one of their great heroes.

Though the Alexander family, some of whose lands it appropriated, resented founding the town, they compromised when it assumed their name, even donated property for the Market Square. However Belhaven long persisted in common speech; Scottish merchants, come 1752, tried to get the Assembly to adopt that earlier name, but Alexander interests defeated them.

In 1791, the town became part of the District of Columbia and was not retroceded to Virginia till 1846 when the state took over three-fourths of its public indebtedness.

What did its early visitors think of "George Washington's Home Town?" Fortunately many diaries and letters remain; for instance the following is from a Journal kept between Fredericksburg and Boston during April, May, and June 1808: the author, Captain Henry Massie.

> On the 29th of April, Mr. Coleman and myself left little York, in two days we reached Fredericksburg the most extravagantly dear place I ever saw, at 12 o'clock in the night of the first day of May. We took the stage there for Alexandria, breakfasted at Dumfires [sic], and halted at Gaby's [sic] tavern about four o'clock in the evening. Alexandria is a very handsome town, prettily situated on the banks of the Potomac, which is there one mile and a quarter wide. The commerce of the place is diffused in many parts of the globe, but more particularly to the West Indies and the northern seaport towns of America. Flour appears to be the principal article of exportation, in return they receive groceries of various kinds, such as sugar, salt, rum, brandy, etc. The streets of Alexandria intersect each other at right angles, they are well paved, of an extensive width, and kept perfectly clean.
>
> There is here open every morning an abundantly supplied market with all kinds of meats, and every species of vegetables. The buildings are chiefly of brick, some of them very stately and elegant. The banks are kept in houses quite magnificent.
>
> The embargo has very much checked and restrained the active, and enterprising commercial spirit which has prevailed here in a very high degree. The wharves are crowded with vessels of different sizes, many of which are heavily laden for an immediate departure — when circumstances will permit. From Alexandria to Washington by land is eight miles, the distance by water six and a half, which may be sailed in 30 minutes — with the sail of breeze that prevails every day from the hours of eleven ante meridian until sunset.

Captain Enoch G. Parrott of Portsmouth, New Hampshire, headed a letter to his wife: "Alexandria, November 4th 1809" and noted:

> Mr. Joshua Yeaton is very polite to me and takes particular pains to render time pleasant. This is the most pleasant town in the southern states, regularly plan'd pleasantly situated, kept very clean. Built in squares, principally of Brick. The Capitol [sic] City of Washington in sight on the opposite side of the river has a pleasant effect. Shall take a turn there some leisurely day.

Do see the Yeaton mansion on Cameron Street opposite the Alexandria Community Y.

Skip now to 1881: the War Between the States is well over, but Alexandria is still in a slump. Perhaps this was for the best because without slaves—their capital—residents were unable to tear down their Georgian and Federal homes and replace them with the most florid period of Victorian architecture. There are many fine early Victorian houses fortunately still occupied and cherished.

The February issue, 1881, of *Scribner's Monthly,* featured these paragraphs:

> Leaving the country road rich in historic memories, we wander back to the town of Alexandria, where linden and sycamore trees shade a little broken-backed street, which dropping suddenly down a hill, ends in the river; two large and somber warehouses, gradually going the way of brick and stone left to care for itself, guard its river end. Their great dimensions are impressive, and suggest the rich stores of tobacco and flour which they formerly contained. Here, along the river front, one can see the high-water marks of a great trade ebbed forever away.
>
> It takes but little imagination to repeople these silent streets along the Potomac, guarded still by their antiquated guns, with the busy motley crowd they once knew. Foreign ships were constantly discharging their cargoes and taking on fresh ones. Their masts showed above the warehouses, and the vista at the end of the street was fairly choked up by a network of cordage and tapering spars. In the noisy crowd, the harsh Dutch and English speech was mingled with the mellower accents of France and Spain. The costumes were as different as the nations.

What a contrast to that unknown author's piece and *Spring Recess* by Marni Davis Wood in the May 1937 issue of *American Home.* Both painter and author, she wrote: "From the basin, with its circling cherry trees, and down the Memorial Parkway to Alexandria." (No Chamber of Commerce sign there then.)

> Take the time in Alexandria to drive around the side streets and see the little houses painted chartreuse and dusty pink, or pale blue with olive green trim, gray blue with chocolate trim. Gay colored houses with gay colored occupants spilling out of them beside enormous boxwoods sprawling around the doorways. A cantaloupe colored front and a watermelon pink end with a dusky matron in lemon yellow standing barefoot in her doorway; a curious tiny half-house of dark red brick with glistening white trim, huge boxwood in the garden and a towering star magnolia.

Doubtless that "curious half-house" was one of Old Town's unique "flounder houses." Windows in the founding days were taxed, glass costly. Homes were hard to heat, so usually, the north wall was windowless. In order to satisfy the stipulation (1749) of building within two years, such houses generally were built on back of the lot and, as owners prospered, stately brick mansions were attached in front. All part of Alexandria's special ambience.

No less a literary light than Alec Waugh paid his tribute to the city in a piece titled "London on the Potomac" which appeared in *National Review* in 1968. He wrote (in part):

> On both sides of Jefferson Davis Highway there is a proliferation of everything that is necessary to and unpleasant about progress—motels, factories, chimney stacks, garages, pizza joints, high concrete barracks, a litter of ugliness and confusion, a jungle of intertwining highroads. Old Alexandria has been very lucky.
>
> This was not by any means the first time that I had been there. I have the good luck to have a number of friends in Old Town. But those visits had been short and I had put up in a hotel. This time I stayed three months and rented what is here called a "carriage house," and in London a "mews studio." It was once, I suppose, a barn for hay and harness, where the grooms slept possibly. You get quite a different view of a town when you do your own marketing instead of ringing up room service, and take your own shirts to the laundry instead of handing them to the hall porter.
>
> I knew when I signed that lease that by the time it expired in October I should have acquired an entirely new insight into Alexandria. I suspected that I was on the brink of a new experience, but that experience, when it came, was altogether different from what I had expected.
>
> During that "long hot summer"—and oh, how hot it was—I found myself enchantingly transported to the London of the early Twenties. As I walked back at night under the trees, past those Georgian houses, and saw behind half-drawn curtains bright interiors of bookshelves, pictures,

mirrors and polished furniture—the proof that quiet cultured people were leading their quiet cultured lives—I remembered how more than forty years ago in London I had walked past just such houses to the tube or bus or taxi that would take me home.

London is not like that any more, and in the city of my birth I find myself looking for pockets of resistance in this club, that restaurant, and the other *cul de sac.*

But here, in this city that was built by Englishmen who, as Alice Duer Miller pointed out in her *White Cliffs of Dover,* were never more English than when they refused to be pushed around by Englishmen, I found myself in the London of Aldous Huxley, Michael Arlen, John Galsworthy and my brother's early novels.

Note: Waugh's tribute to Alexandria was penned prior to the current intense local devotion to Scottishness promoted by the Y's famed Christmas Walks. No Cameron-plaided bagpipers in Alexandria that hot summer.

A recent president of Yale University observed how we used to see "with the mind's eye" and today, perhaps due to television, see with "the eye's mind." Surely splendid pictures in Karen Harvey's book will enrich the latter. The young author includes several never published before, including Elliots' tall house on South Fairfax Street beside the Old Presbyterian Meeting House and just around the corner from Waugh's carriage house in the 200 block of Wolfe Street.

Let's get acquainted.

Jean Elliot

I. PEOPLE

George Washington painted in 1776 by Charles Willson Peale.

Courtesy of Mount Vernon Ladies' Association

Alexandria is truly a city with a "past." Every facet reflects the beginnings of this country and the growth that brings it to the present day. Names of people associated with Alexandria have a familiar ring even to those who have never set foot inside its boundaries. George Washington and Robert E. Lee were Alexandrians. Generals Braddock and Lafayette left their marks upon the city. Henry Clay, John Calhoun, and Daniel Webster were frequent visitors. The somewhat lesser known names of George Mason, George Johnston, Henry "Light Horse Harry" Lee, General Montgomery Corse, and Kate Waller Barrett are people whose influence has reached far. These are but a few of the people who made Alexandria what it is today. Many others helped shape the city. Some are familiar names to Alexandrians, some are not.

Were it not for an innocent oversight, Alexandria could well bear the name of Brentville or Brenton instead of the name it carries today in honor of the Alexander family. In 1654 Margaret Brent, then of Maryland, received a grant of seven hundred acres on the Potomac above Hunting creek. This tract was included in the Howsing Patent of six thousand acres received by Robert Howsing in 1669. Having little interest in the land, Howsing sold the patent to John Alexander in November of that year at a price amounting to one pound of tobacco per acre. The error of the overlapping land went undiscovered for many years. However, the heirs of John Alexander were obliged to reimburse Mistress Brent's descendants. As if paying twice were not agony enough, the price set by the Brents was fifteen pounds of tobacco per acre, fifteen times the original cost.

John Alexander was the first prominent settler of the area which became known as Alexander land. He built a home in 1675 near what is now Four Mile Run. At the time of his death in 1677 his estate was inherited by his sons, Philip and Robert. Philip's portion was the lower region, which would become

Alexandria. Part of this land was leased to Thomas Pearson and eventually passed through family hands to Hugh West, Sr. Upon this land the tobacco warehouse known as Hunting Creek Warehouse was built around 1730. The spot, called West's Point, was wisely chosen by three Scottish settlers, William Ramsay, John Carlyle, and John Pagan. The deep water and good approach made an ideal harbor on the Potomac.

Hunting Creek Warehouse stood at the end of what is now Oronoco Street. Before long a few small cabins dotted the area, and the primarily Scottish settlers named their small community Belhaven in honor of the Earl of Belhaven of Scotland. In 1748 the General Assembly at Williamsburg acted upon petitions for a town to be developed on land surrounding the warehouse. The town was to be built upon a sixty acre tract owned by the heirs of John Alexander. Although this plan met with some opposition, the Authorization Act stood, and eleven trustees were appointed to determine the new town's future.

By official act the name of Belhaven was dropped in preference to the name honoring the Alexander family. Despite objections of a few loyal Scots, the little settlement around the warehouse became known as Alexandria. Plans were formulated to survey the land and divide it into squares with half acre lots. These were to be auctioned publicly as soon as time permitted. Surveying quickly got underway and seventeen-year-old George Washington assisted with the project. By the summer of 1749 plans were completed, and on July 13 the public auction took place.

John Dalton purchased the first lot, number 36, on the northwest corner of Cameron and Water Streets, acquiring the adjoining property later in the bidding. On that day prices ranged from approximately 69 dollars to 245 dollars. Sales went for considerably less the second day, although spirits remained high. Forty-one of the eighty-four lots were sold. It was stipulated that no man could purchase more than two lots from the initial auctions. In addition to Dalton's acquisitions, double purchases were made by foresighted men such as John Carlyle, William Ramsay, and Lawrence Washington.

The new landowners began immediately to build upon the half acres. A regulation in the Founding Act specified construction must begin within two years. However, no prodding was necessary to spur them to action. William Ramsay brought his home by barge from Dumfries and placed it on lot number 47 long before others were able to gather their stone or wood and begin to build. John Dalton had a clapboard house completed within three years, and Carlyle's mansion-like home graced two lots of Fairfax Street by 1752. The homes of Ramsay and Carlyle can be seen today. On Dalton's property stands the Jonah Thompson house. One wing of the brick edifice possibly encases the original Dalton home.

William Ramsay became Alexandria's first and only Lord Mayor. He was elected in 1761, adding that office to his long list of positions as public servant in the new town. One of Ramsay's eight children, Dennis, also served as mayor of the town. It was Dennis who had the honor of addressing General Washington as he passed through Alexandria on the way to his inauguration as President of the United States in 1789. "Light Horse Harry" Lee collaborated on the speech.

Ann McCarty, William Ramsay's wife, has her own place in history. She raised over seventy-five thousand dollars for aid to the Continental Army, and was said to have been called the "greatest patriot." She died in 1795, less than two months after her husband. Both were greatly mourned by the citizens of Alexandria, including their good friend, George Washington.

John Carlyle, along with William Ramsay and John Pagan, lived in Dumfries as agents for a Scottish shipping firm when the advantages of the Hunting Creek Warehouse site were determined and the move was made to the new location up the Potomac. In 1744 Carlyle was in business with Ramsay, trading out of Belhaven. He also was a partner in the mercantile and shipping firm of Carlyle and Dalton, which became one of the most important shipping firms in the new port. His stately home was the scene of numerous parties and gatherings and was for years considered the town's social hub. Its halls echoed with the voices of men such as Washington, Lafayette, Franklin, John Paul Jones, Jefferson, John Marshall, and Aaron Burr.

The Carlyle House was headquarters for Major General Edward Braddock in 1755 when the colonies were under threat of attack from

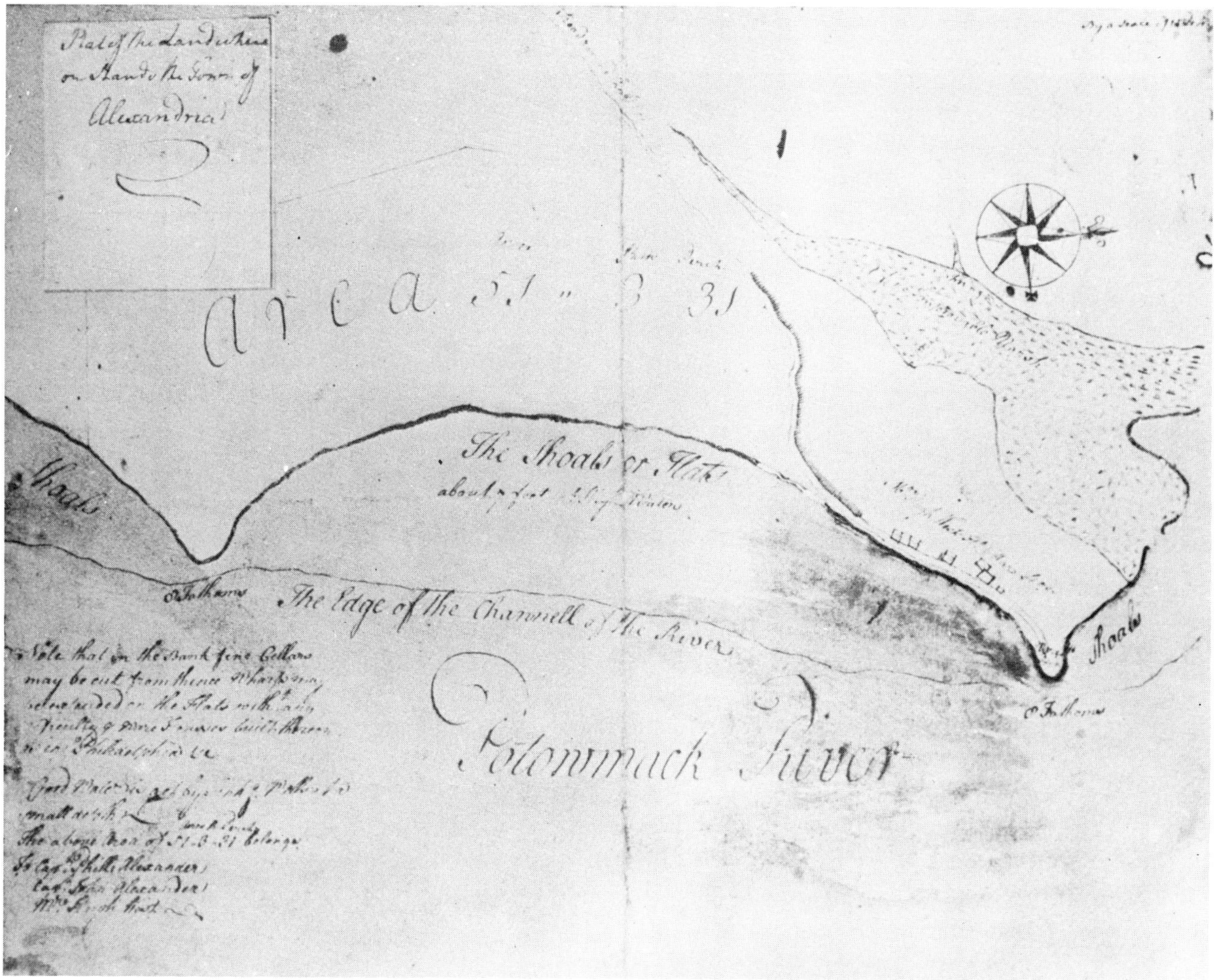

Survey of Belhaven by George Washington (1748).

Courtesy of National Archives

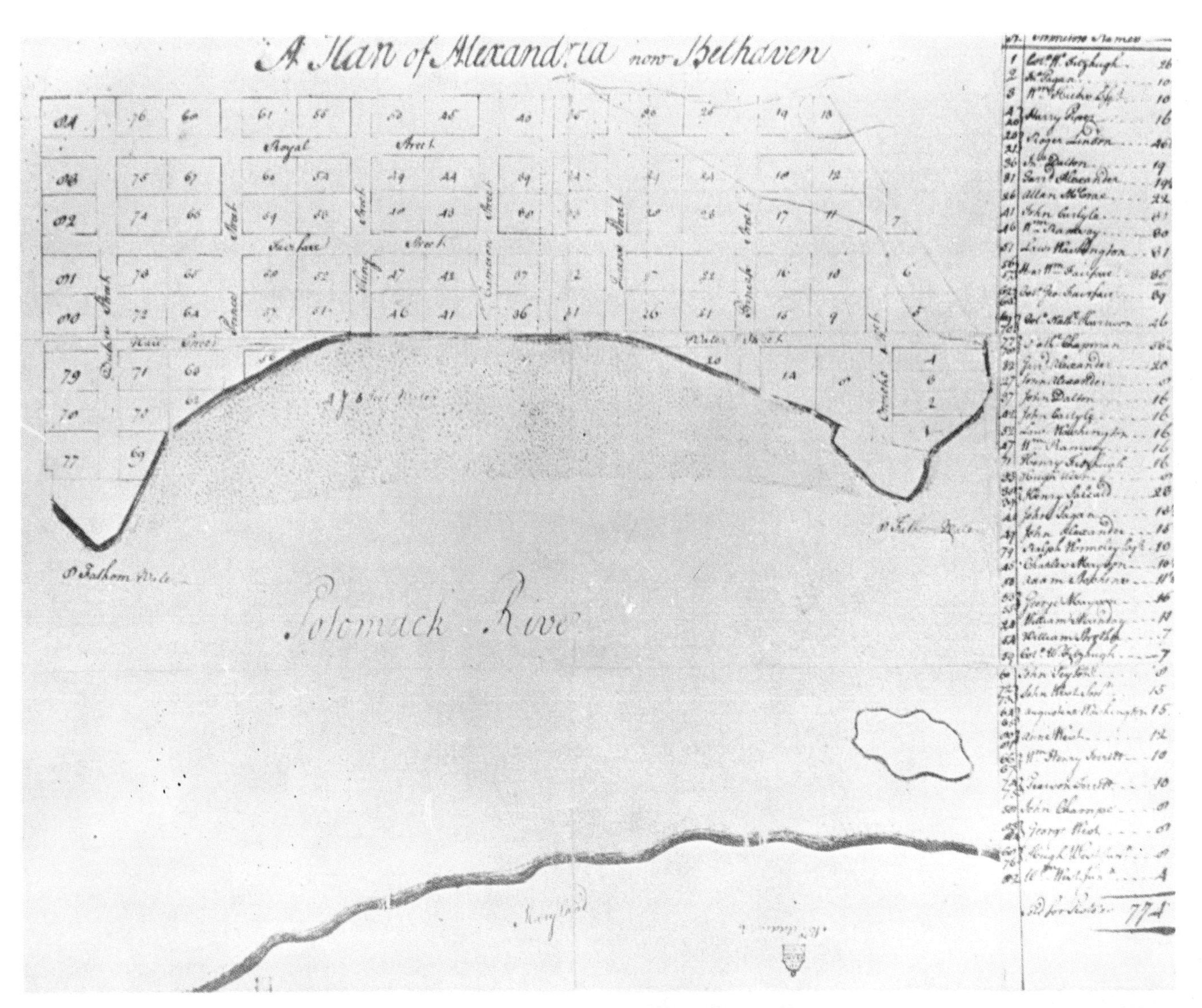

George Washington's plan for Alexandria, drawn in 1749. The numbered squares represent the eighty-four half acre lots put up for auction in July. To the right are the names of the new landowners with the number of the lot purchased.

Courtesy of National Archives

Ann Pamela Cunningham, granddaughter of John Dalton, was founder and first regent of Mount Vernon Ladies' Association, the organization responsible for the restoration and preservation of the historic estate.

Courtesy of Mount Vernon Ladies' Association

Mount Vernon, the Washington family estate, overlooks the Potomac at a point nine miles south of Alexandria. The present structure began as a one and a half story cottage built in the 1730s by George Washington's father, Augustine. Only eleven years old when his father died, George Washington lived with his mother in Fredericksburg, Virginia, though frequently visiting his half-brother Lawrence at Mount Vernon. He became a permanent resident of the plantation after Lawrence's death in 1754, coming into possession of the property seven years later when Lawrence's widow, Anne, died. Mount Vernon was home to this country's first President until his death in 1799—forty-five years of ever strengthening ties to the nearby town of Alexandria. This snow scene shows the plantation house in the 1960s.

Photo by Ben T. Boogher, Jr.

the French Canadians and the Ohio Valley Indians. After discussing defense plans with the governors of Maryland, Massachusetts, New York, Pennsylvania, and Virginia, Braddock determined that a steep tax was necessary to pay for his expedition. His recommendation to the mother country led to the hated Stamp Act, the spark that touched off the Revolution.

While Braddock's troops waited in camp outside Alexandria, Washington drilled his men in Market Square. Soon the armies marched off to attack Fort Duquesne, a campaign which failed and cost Braddock his life.

The years preceding the Revolution proved years of growth for Alexandria. A courthouse was built in 1753 and the jail, stocks, and whipping post were used when needed. By the end of 1754 other public buildings were under construction, and by 1759 Town Hall was erected in Market Square. In this building the first grammar school began in a small space on the lower floor. Four streets were added in 1763—Wilkes, Wolfe, Pitt, and St. Asaph.

Plans for construction of a church began in 1767, and six years later Christ Church was completed. In 1774, the Presbyterian Church opened its doors and the Friendship Fire Company was formed. The town rapidly grew in importance as a popular seaport.

Rumblings of war were heard early in Alexandria. George Johnston, a town trustee, loudly protested the tyranny of England. It was he who inspired Patrick Henry's oratory which sparked the fury of so many colonists. George Mason of Gunston Hall, another trustee, prepared the Fairfax Resolves, a document of human rights that cried out for free government. As the colonists grew more and more restless they looked to one man in particular for leadership, and that man was George Washington of Alexandria.

Washington had been drilling volunteer companies of militia for some time before the Continental Army was formed. In 1774 he appeared at the First Continental Congress in Philadelphia in full uniform and was recognized by Patrick Henry as one of the greatest men present. By June of 1775, the Congress authorized the formation of the Army and appointed Washington Commander-in-Chief. This was the beginning of Washington's long absence from Alexandria as he led the struggle for independence.

Of the thirteen colonies, Virginia and Massachusetts played leading roles in the Revolution. Virginia contributed fifteen infantry regiments which fought at Trenton, Brandywine, Germantown, and Monmouth. Though Alexandria sent her men into battle, the city played only a small part in the fight for independence. Citizens of the town feared attack along the Potomac and were constantly aware of the need to defend themselves. In 1781 "Light Horse Harry" Lee reported to Virginia Governor Thomas Jefferson that an unsuccessful attempt had been made by the British to capture Alexandria. Later that year a nearby farm was burned and enemy ships were reported opposite Hooe's Ferry and at Mount Vernon. In a communication to the Governor the request was made to keep at home the 114 men scheduled to leave for battlefields.

In addition to Major General "Light Horse Harry" Lee, three other military leaders returned from war to make Alexandria their home. James Hendricks, John Fitzgerald, and Charles Simms, all field grade officers, served terms as mayor, Hendricks in 1781 and Fitzgerald in 1787. Simms had the dubious honor of holding the office when the British occupied Alexandria in August of 1814.

Alexandrians joyfully welcomed home their hero in 1783. Washington had been away more than eight years. The city had weathered a smallpox epidemic in addition to severe shortages of imported foods, in particular the essential commodity, salt. Now the town was ready to move ahead. Because of the development of the brick industry, bigger and stronger structures were erected. Captain Bathurst Daingerfield put up two large brick homes in the western portion of Alexandria exemplifying the expansion "out of town." The weekly newspaper founded in 1784—*Virginia Journal and Alexandria Advertiser*—printed local occurrences and advertised new businesses. The town was doing well in 1789 when the citizens watched their own favorite son take office as the first President of the new country.

An important decision for Congress was choosing a location for the nation's capital. Virginia delegate Major General Lee suggested a site along the Potomac. Thomas Jefferson specifically proposed Shooter's Hill as an ideal spot for the Capitol building. In 1790 Congress passed the Residence Act which set certain boundary regulations along the Potomac, but gave the President choice of the exact spot for the Federal district. The regulation called for an area ten miles square. It was Washington's decision to include Alexandria within the district limits but with the proviso that no public buildings be erected west of the Potomac. Surveying began by drawing a line from the Alexandria Courthouse to Hunting Creek, and on April 15, 1791, Jones Point was ceremoniously declared the first corner of the new Federal City. Ten years later Alexandria became the responsibility of the United States Congress, and Virginia could no longer claim the community on the Potomac as one of its cities. From 1801 to 1846, Alexandria, District of Columbia, belonged to the federal government.

During the last decade of the 1700s the town flourished. Financial transactions were facilitated when the Alexandria Bank opened in 1792, and the founding of the Library Company in 1794 offered new cultural opportunities. However, the century ended sadly when the honored and respected citizen, George Washington, died on December 16, 1799. With him at Mt. Vernon were Dr. James Craik and the young doctors Elisha Cullen Dick and William Brown. Martha and the trusted servant Christopher were by his side, as was Tobias Lear, whose account of the fateful night touches all who are part of the country Washington loved.

Ramsay House, 221 King Street, as it looked in the 1920s. It is now beautifully restored and used as the Tourist Council office.

Courtesy of Charles Sampson

Back of Ramsay House and entrance to Tourist Council. Photo taken in the spring of 1974.

Courtesy of Alexandria Tourist Council

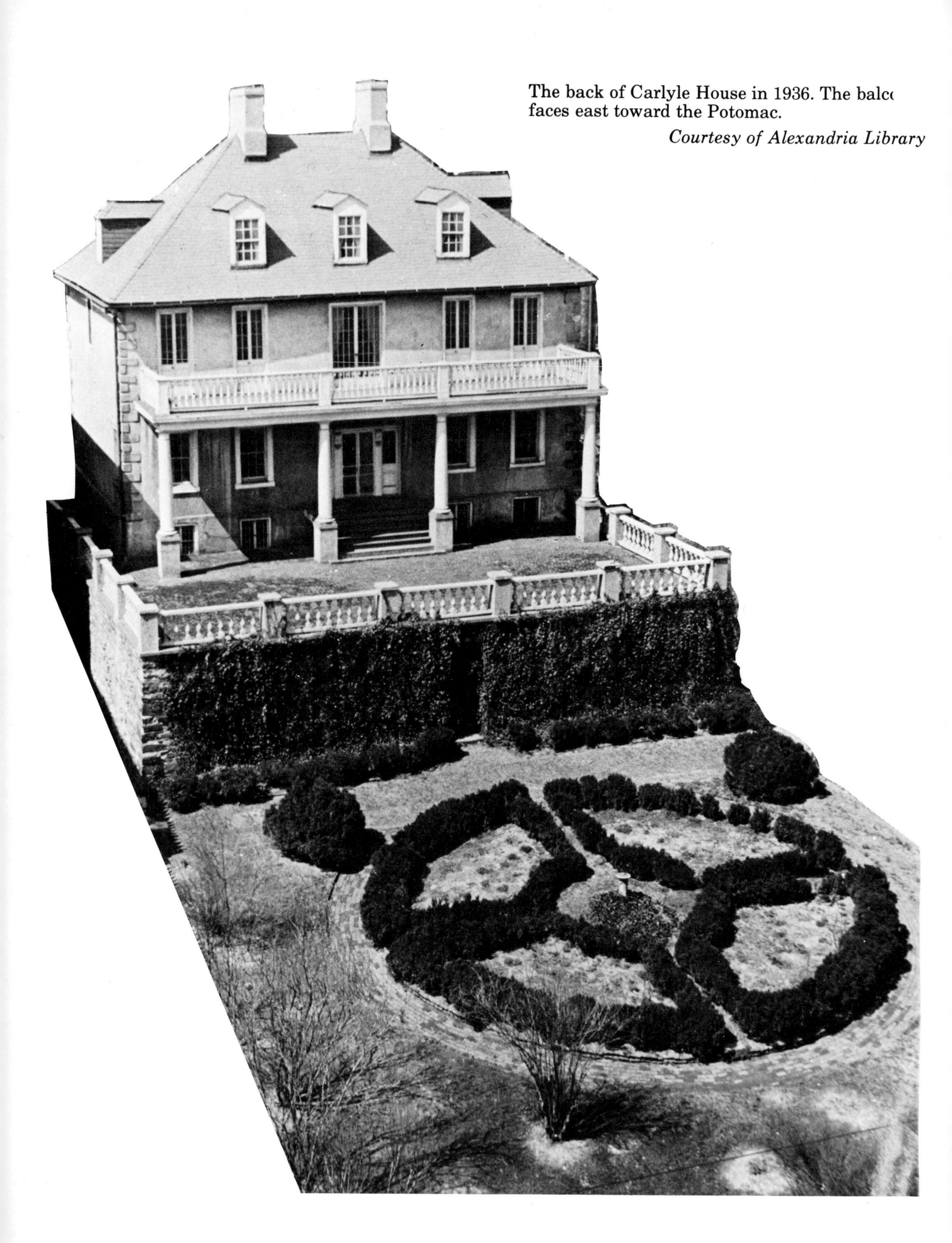

The back of Carlyle House in 1936. The balc
faces east toward the Potomac.

Courtesy of Alexandria Library

Carlyle House after restoration in May 1976.
Photo by Ross Stansfield

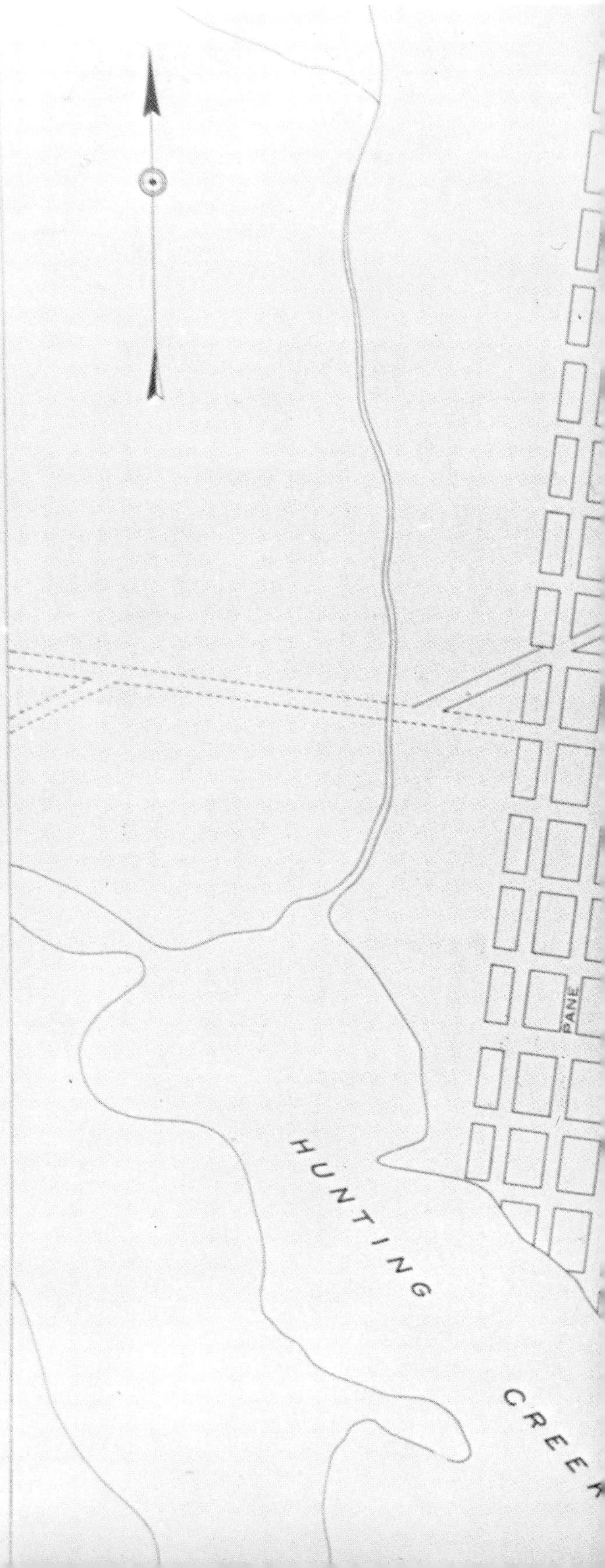

Localities associated with George Washington. The 1749 plan extended from Royal to the river, (the land area now Union Street and part of Lee was filled in later) and from Oronoco south to Duke. Acreage owned by Margaret Brent ran west along Hunting Creek for about one mile and north to Queen Street.

Courtesy of National Archives

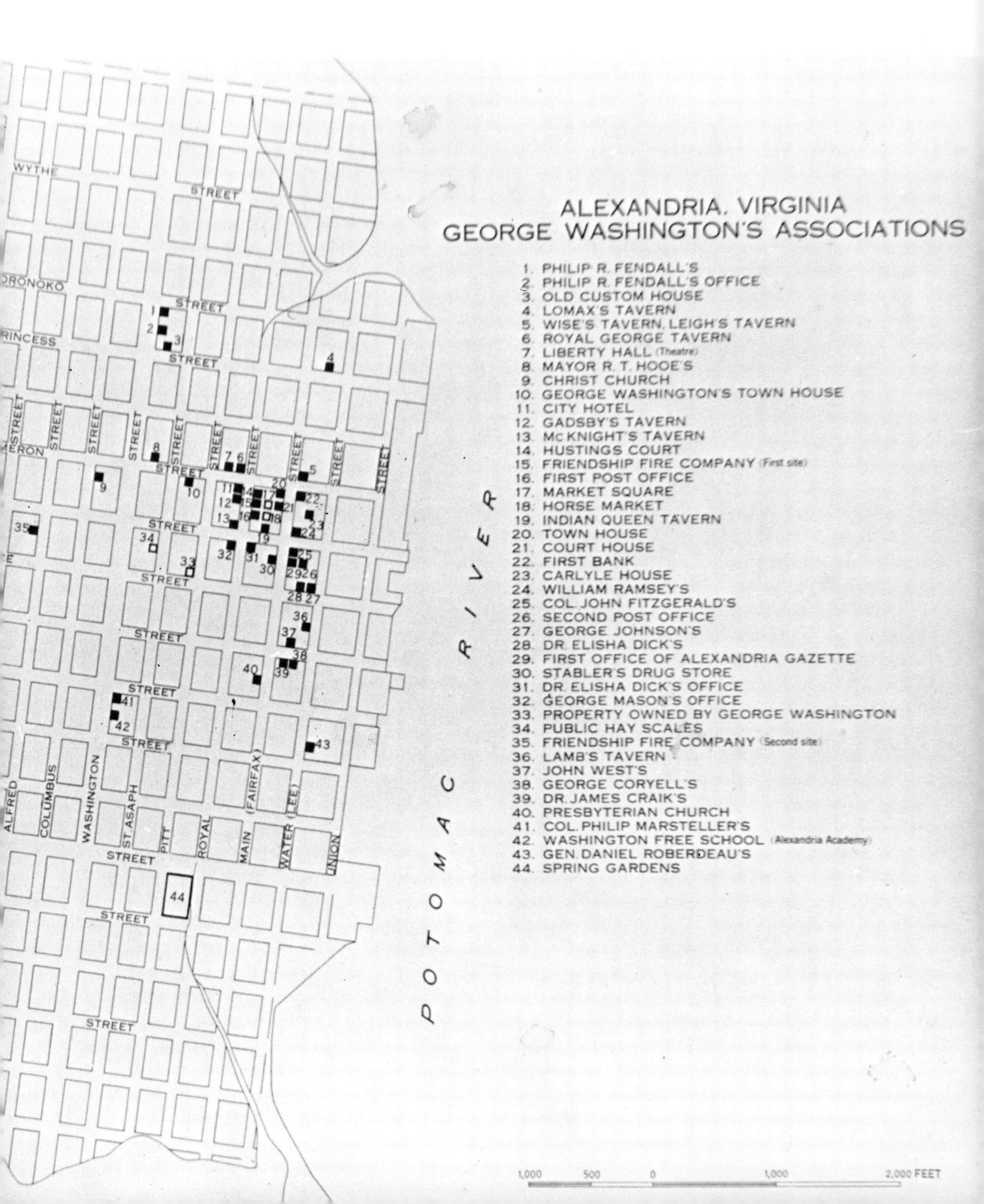

ALEXANDRIA, VIRGINIA
GEORGE WASHINGTON'S ASSOCIATIONS
1. PHILIP R. FENDALL'S
2. PHILIP R. FENDALL'S OFFICE
3. OLD CUSTOM HOUSE
4. LOMAX'S TAVERN
5. WISE'S TAVERN, LEIGH'S TAVERN
6. ROYAL GEORGE TAVERN
7. LIBERTY HALL (Theatre)
8. MAYOR R. T. HOOE'S
9. CHRIST CHURCH
10. GEORGE WASHINGTON'S TOWN HOUSE
11. CITY HOTEL
12. GADSBY'S TAVERN
13. McKNIGHT'S TAVERN
14. HUSTINGS COURT
15. FRIENDSHIP FIRE COMPANY (First site)
16. FIRST POST OFFICE
17. MARKET SQUARE
18. HORSE MARKET
19. INDIAN QUEEN TAVERN
20. TOWN HOUSE
21. COURT HOUSE
22. FIRST BANK
23. CARLYLE HOUSE
24. WILLIAM RAMSEY'S
25. COL. JOHN FITZGERALD'S
26. SECOND POST OFFICE
27. GEORGE JOHNSON'S
28. DR. ELISHA DICK'S
29. FIRST OFFICE OF ALEXANDRIA GAZETTE
30. STABLER'S DRUG STORE
31. DR. ELISHA DICK'S OFFICE
32. GEORGE MASON'S OFFICE
33. PROPERTY OWNED BY GEORGE WASHINGTON
34. PUBLIC HAY SCALES
35. FRIENDSHIP FIRE COMPANY (Second site)
36. LAMB'S TAVERN
37. JOHN WEST'S
38. GEORGE CORYELL'S
39. DR. JAMES CRAIK'S
40. PRESBYTERIAN CHURCH
41. COL. PHILIP MARSTELLER'S
42. WASHINGTON FREE SCHOOL (Alexandria Academy)
43. GEN. DANIEL ROBERDEAU'S
44. SPRING GARDENS
WYTHE
STREET
ORONOKO
STREET
RINCESS
STREET
MERON
STREET
ALFRED
COLUMBUS
WASHINGTON
ST. ASAPH
PITT
ROYAL
(FAIRFAX)
MAIN
WATER (LEE)
UNION
POTOMAC RIVER
1,000 500 0 1,000 2,000 FEET

THE ALEXANDRIA WATER COMPANY

Benjamin Hallowell is best known in Alexandria as the Quaker school teacher. However, his direct involvement with the formation of the Alexandria Water Company is of equal importance as one of his many contributions to the growth and development of the city. Until the mid-1800s Alexandria obtained water from street corner wells and diagonal pumps. Several options were investigated as possible water sources, but none seemed acceptable solutions to the problem. The Chesapeake and Ohio Canal was under construction and served as a possible answer. Neither the canal nor a reservoir on the Potomac could supply pure drinking water. Hallowell's plan was to transport water from Cameron Run to the top of Shooter's Hill. From there the water would pass by gravity through Alexandria homes and out to the Potomac.

Already in existence, Cameron Mill was the ideal spot from which to draw the city's water. In 1849, Robert French Roberts came to Alexandria from New Jersey. He purchased Cameron Farm on which stood the Cameron Mill, believed to have been built during the time of George Washington. The Roberts family involvement with the water company went far beyond ownership of the Mill. Robert French

Walter Roberts, member of Roberts family and president of Alexandria Water Company until 1917.

Courtesy of Mary Hunt Roberts

The first order placed for water.

Courtesy of Alexandria Water Company

The millrace.

Courtesy of Mary Hunt Roberts

Cameron Mill in 1889. The mill was built in the late 1700s.

Courtesy of Mary Hunt Roberts

Back of mill with pump house.

Courtesy of Mary Hunt Roberts

Roberts became one of the first directors of the Water Company and his son, Walter Roberts, served as president.

The Alexandria Water Company was incorporated in 1850. A large group of interested citizens met at the Lyceum during the winter of 1850-51 to formulate company policies and plans. Subscriptions were obtained at this time, and Hallowell was elected president. Hallowell accepted the office with the condition that he receive no salary but be permitted to select a qualified engineer for the project. Both requests were granted. Hallowell chose an experienced engineer, Frederick Erdman, to develop details of the project. Erdman's first step was to reject Shooter's Hill and to choose a knoll next to the hill as the point from which water would run. Ground breaking began in 1851, and the first water was conveyed through the pipes to the town on June 15, 1852. From that day Alexandrians had water available in their homes.

The Water Company has experienced various changes in location and ownership since the days of Hallowell and the Roberts family. In 1869, under the presidency of George H. Smoot, the company began enlargement. In 1929 the Alexandria Water Company was purchased by the American Water Works and has remained part of their operation ever since. Originally housed on Prince Street in Old Town, the enterprise now has offices behind the Masonic Temple at the foot of Shooter's Hill. One might say the business has returned home, since it stands in close proximity to the land that was Cameron Farm and the original mill.

Roberts family and friends in front of Cameron farm house.

Courtesy of Mary Hunt Roberts

Members of the Alexandria Water Company in front of Barcroft Dam in 1926. Built by the company between 1913 and 1915, the dam is 67 feet high and 430 feet long. The road in front is Columbia Pike. The photo at right shows Mr. Urban S. Lambert, Water Company member, drinking the pure spring water near the dam.

Courtesy of Ester Lambert

BENJAMIN HALLOWELL

Benjamin Hallowell was an enormously busy person. Few Alexandrians have not been touched in some way by the activities of this man. If one as much as drinks the water in Alexandria he has been affected by the work of this clever and industrious individual.

Alexandria was not Hallowell's place of birth. He arrived in town in 1824 with the intention of opening a school for boys. He was twenty-five years old and newly married. His school was destined to become the most popular school, and he the best known schoolmaster, in Alexandria. Among hundreds of pupils who received the benefits of education from him, the most famous was Robert E. Lee.

Hallowell lived in several different locations, usually running his school from one or more rooms in his home. His success as a teacher was darkened by personal tragedy. Three of his four children died of scarlet fever in less than a month. His wife's poor health forced him to move from his first dwelling on Oronoco Street. Lack of funds kept him from continuing in his second school when the owner of the home, the Widow Hooe, died, and the house was sold in public auction at a price he could not afford.

Benjamin Hallowell.

Courtesy of Mary Hunt Roberts

His energies and interests never waned as he continued to improve and expand every home he lived in. In addition to his architectural talents he was experienced as a surveyor and was made Town Surveyor in 1831. He refused pay for the job, preferring to use the position as a teaching tool for some of his students.

As a Quaker he was a peace-loving man and a believer in freedom. He was a leading force in a society for aid to freed slaves, serving as secretary of a group that was active from 1827 to 1831.

His scholarly mind reached out beyond the classroom. In 1834 Hallowell became president of the Alexandria Lyceum Association, an organization he founded for the intellectual betterment of his contemporaries. It was partially through the efforts of this group that the Alexandria Water Company was later founded. Hallowell was named president of the company (again without pay) and because of his inventiveness and determination Alexandria received its first supply of fresh running water in 1852.

Some Alexandrians are doubtlessly descendants of students of Hallowells. Others have walked through the Lyceum building at some time or used those library facilities which are an outgrowth of the Lyceum Association. It is safe to say that all Alexandrians use the water at some time or another. The residents of Alexandria owe much to the kindly Quaker schoolmaster.

Hallowell's first home and school at 609 Oronoco. The adjacent house at the right is one of the Lee Homes.

Courtesy of Alexandria Library

ALEXANDRIA GAZETTE

The *Alexandria Gazette* proudly flies a flag proclaiming itself to be "America's Oldest Daily." This claim is justified by the fact that the paper can trace its beginnings to 1784, when it was published under the name of the *Virginia Journal and Alexandria Advertiser.* Established by George Richards, it was then a weekly. By 1797 the paper was published as a daily under another name. Samuel Snowden acquired it in 1800 along with another local publication. He remained owner and editor until 1831 when his son Edgar succeeded him. Edgar was forced to publish an underground newspaper during the Civil War and was witness to the fire which destroyed the *Gazette* office on Prince Street.

In 1911 the *Gazette* passed from the hands of the Snowden family. Charles C. Carlin, Sr., became the controlling stockholder. Under his leadership and that of his son, the *Gazette* flourished as Alexandria's oldest newspaper. When Charles C. Carlin, Jr., died in 1966 his wife, Sarah S. Carlin, became president and editor. She sold the paper to the State-Record Company, Columbia, South Carolina, in October 1973. It has remained a part of that corporation.

The Alexandria Gazette
Gazette Home On Prince Street . . .
Alexandria Gazette
...From 1857 To Outbreak Of War Between States

Old *Gazette* building before moving to 317 King Street. Since 1965 the *Gazette* has operated from 717 St. Asaph Street.

*Courtesy of the **Gazette***

Edgar Snowden. In addition to his association with the *Gazette,* Snowden was mayor from 1839 to 1843 and the first delegate sent to the Virginia Assembly when the town was ceded back to the state.

*Courtesy of the **Gazette***

STABLER-LEADBEATER APOTHECARY

The story begins in 1792 when Edward Stabler borrowed one hundred pounds to purchase stock for an apothecary shop. The tale has no date to mark its ending since the Apothecary Shop can be visited today; descendants of the original owners still reside in Alexandria.

Stabler's shop prospered during its first year and has remained a time-honored landmark. George Washington often stopped to chat with the proprietor and to purchase medicines and other items necessary for household welfare. Martha Washington continued dealings there after her husband's death. Still in existence is a note from her written in 1802 requesting that a quart of Stabler's best castor oil be sent to Mt. Vernon.

Washington is not the only famous name associated with the gathering place. Here Robert E. Lee first heard the news of John Brown's raid and received his orders to proceed to Harper's Ferry. The messenger had been told the shop was one place where Lee might be found.

A letter written in 1818 tells of George Washington Parke Curtis' transactions with the owner. Other notes from Nelly Curtis (Mrs. Lawrence Lewis) have also been preserved.

At another time, shortly before the Civil War, it became the custom of such illustrious personages as Henry Clay, John Calhoun, and Daniel Webster to meet at the Fairfax Street shop to discuss issues of the day while waiting to board a ferry to Washington. This practice grew as a result of numerous dinner parties given by Phineas P. Janney, a brother-in-law of Mary Hartshorne, for these men and other notables.

Over the years the enterprise expanded to meet the growing demands of a thriving town. New shops in the same block opened as the family added wholesale outlets and drug manufacturing to the prosperous retail trade. The business always remained in the hands of the same family. The Stabler and Leadbeater names were joined when John Leadbeater married Mary Stabler, Edward and Mary's daughter, and became partner. A plaque in the rear lists the dates and name changes that occurred with the passage of time.

In 1933 the Apothecary Shop closed its doors after almost a century and a half of service. However, its historic value was recognized immediately both by the community and the American Pharmaceutical Society. The entire stock, including three of the original purchases made by Edward Stabler, has been preserved. Through the efforts of the Landmark Society, the renovated shop reopened in 1934 as a museum. Edward Stabler's story continues today in its original setting, a place where young and old can momentarily step back into the past.

Jack Leadbeater about 1899, on the corner of Prince and Pitt Streets.

Courtesy of Eleanor Leadbeater

Edward Stabler.
Courtesy of Eleanor Leadbeater

Mary Hartshorne Stabler.
Courtesy of Eleanor Leadbeater

A Stabler descendant, Howard Bloomer, III, visiting the apothecary shop in 1930 and 1970.

Courtesy of the ***Gazette***

Eleanor Leadbeater and friend outside Gadsby's in the 1940s.

Courtesy of Eleanor Leadbeater

Don Slaugh, current curator of Apothecary.

Photo by Ross Stansfield
Courtesy of ***Alexandria Port Packet***

Leadbeater Drug Corporation, no longer in existence. This is one of the establishments opened during its period of expansion.

Courtesy of Alexandria Library

Robert E. Lee.

Courtesy of Lee-Fendall House

THE LEES

The Lees of Virginia occupied numerous residences in Alexandria. In addition to the Lee Fendall House and Lee's boyhood home, there exist the houses associated with Edmund Jennings Lee (428 North Washington), Henry Lee (611 Cameron), Charles Lee (407 North Washington), and others. The Duvall House and Lloyd House also claim Lee family connections.

Anne Lee, descendant of Robert E. Lee, seated at spinning wheel of her ancestor Lucy Grymos Lee, mother of "Light Horse Harry." Behind her is a portrait of Richard Henry Lee, one of two Lee brothers who signed the Declaration of Independence. Lee family possessions can be viewed in the Lee-Fendall House.

Photo by Ross Stansfield

The boyhood home of Robert E. Lee, 607 Oronoco Street, was twice the residence of young Robert, once as a child and later as a young man about to leave for West Point. The house adjoins the first home and school of Benjamin Hallowell.

Courtesy of Alexandria Tourist Council

Frances Shively welcomes the dark-haired "first-footer" to the Lee-Fendall house (Oronoco Street entrance) for the celebration of Hogmanay on New Year's Eve 1975. Traditionally, the first person to set foot across the threshold on "Old Year's Night" must be tall and dark-haired. Gifts are then exchanged and the house blessed. The Alexandria Tourist Council sponsors this happy Scottish custom which includes the Alexandria Pipes and Drums as an integral part of the festivities.

Photo by Ross Stansfield

Lee-Fendall House, 429 North Washington Street, was the home of twenty-one Lees and is now a shrine to Major General Henry "Light Horse Harry" Lee. The house was built by Philip Richard Fendall in 1785. Himself a Lee descendant, his three marriages were to Lee women.

Courtesy of Alexandria Tourist Council

THE BARRETT FAMILY

One of the beautiful people of Alexandria is Kate Waller Barrett. Dr. Barrett was not born in Alexandria, but made it her home for thirty years and left a heritage of love and compassion. Known primarily as co-founder of the National Florence Crittenton Mission, her list of activities and achievements range from local to international levels. The Alexandria Library is named in honor of this woman who spent her life increasing social awareness and helping others not as fortunate as herself.

Kate Waller's family home was on the banks of the Potomac a short distance south of Alexandria. She was born there in 1857, and married the Reverend Robert Barrett when she was nineteen. Her only formal education was the two years spent at the Arlington Institute for Girls in Alexandria. However, as wife and mother she attended medical school and received her medical degree from the Woman's Medical College in Altanta, Georgia. She never practiced medicine, but used her knowledge as a means of gaining insight into the complicated world with which she worked. At her death in 1925 the flag over the Richmond Capitol was flown at half-mast, an honor distinguished by the fact she was the first woman to be so recognized.

The eldest Barrett son, Robert South Barrett (1877-1959), organized a local branch of the Crittenton Mission in 1933. His name is known through his association with the library, *Gazette,* and Boys' Club. In addition, he established a private foundation that supports church work, welfare programs, and educational and cultural charities.

A school is named for another son, Charles Dodson Barrett, a Major General in the United States Marine Corps, killed in the South Pacific in 1943.

The Kate Waller Barrett House at 408 Duke Street in 1960.

Courtesy of Mrs. Milton Greenland

Taylor Burke, current president of Burke and Herbert Bank.

Photo by Ross Stansfield

Started as a private financial house and managed as a partnership, the Burke and Herbert Bank still follows the principles of the old form of banking. Bank accounts use names, not numbers, and records are kept in old-fashioned ledgers rather than computer print-outs.

Photo by Ross Stansfield

This house at 619 South Lee Street, was the Snowden family home from 1842 to 1912. For years the residence of Justice Hugo Black, the inset shows his daughter, Josephine, after her wedding in their home.

Courtesy of Edith Snowden
Photo by Ben T. Boogher, Jr.

Your devoted Dad
Feb 22 1953

President Eisenhower with Mayor Marshall Beverley visiting Christ Church in 1954.

Courtesy of Marshall Beverley

President Herbert Hoover in town for dedication of George Washington Parkway, which opened to Mount Vernon in 1932. Beside car, left to right, are Governor John G. Pollard, Mrs. Hoover, President Hoover, Mr. William A. Smoot, and Mayor Edmund F. Ticer.

Courtesy of Mr. and Mrs. Stanley King

Justice William O. Douglass, left, at wedding of Josephine Black and Mario Pesaresi.

Photo by Ben T. Boogher, Jr.

President William H. Taft in front of Congressman Charles Carlin's home at 211 North Washington Street, taken during the 1910 George Washington Birthday Parade. Left to right are Carlin, Taft, "Uncle Joe" Cannon (Speaker of the House), Senator Claude Swanson, and Vice President James S. Sherman.

Courtesy of Laurence Fawcett

Queen Rambai of Siam, center right, with Mrs. Herbert Hoover, center left, visiting Mount Vernon during 1931 trip to United States. The King is second from left with camera.

Courtesy of Laura Southard

Picture on the steps of Gadsby's includes Governor Pollard, his son and son's fiancee, Mr. Carroll Pierce, Mr. Weil, Mr. Harry Kirk, and Mayor Ticer.

Courtesy of Mr. and Mrs. Stanley King

Gerald Ford with Marshall Beverley at Friendship Firehouse in 1974.

Photo by Ross Stansfield

R. J. Sweeney, Senator James Buckley, Senator Harry F. Byrd, Jr., Colonel Wilfred Smith, and Friendship Fire Company president Marshall Beverley.

Photo by Ross Stansfield

Mr. William Robert Adam escorts First Lady Betty Ford into Gadsby's Tavern, October 14, 1975.

Photo by Ross Stansfield

William F. Hellmuth, unofficial historian of Fire Department.

Courtesy of Charles Sampson

Nettie Allen Voges, historian and author of *Old Alexandria.*

Photo by Ross Stansfield
Courtesy of ***Alexandria Port Packet***

Ray Gallagher pointing to his initials and date in the alley of 100 block South St. Asaph.

Photo by Ross Stansfield

Four generations of Alexandrians: Mrs. Robert Lewis Wood, Mrs. George R. Hill, and Mrs. Malcolm Wescott Hill (seated) and baby, George R. Hill, II. Photo taken in 1907.

Courtesy of Anna Hill Stansfield

Alexandria Bicycle Club around 1905. The club's headquarters were on Shooter's Hill.

Courtesy of Charles Sampson

One of the first annual Holly Balls at Belle Haven Country Club, held in 1958.

Photo by Ben T. Boogher, Jr.

Earl Lloyd, first black coach in professional basketball. He is the tallest boy in the back row of this Parker-Gray class photo, circa 1944.

Courtesy of Helen Day

Three Alexandria citizens around 1915. The gentleman in the middle is Harry Entwisle.

Courtesy of Charles Sampson

William R. A. Kleysteuber, 401 Newton Avenue, Potomac, was twice mayor of Potomac and served two terms as a member of the Potomac town council. He was also affiliated with the Masonic Order. He was instrumental in incorporating Potomac into Alexandria and starting the Fire Department.

Courtesy of Peggy Kleysteuber

Charles Sampson. Member of the Alexandria Fire Department from 1937 to 1975, he was battalion chief of the Department from 1950 until his retirement.

Courtesy of Charles Sampson

George Washington's review of the troops in front of Gadsby's, November 8, 1975.

Photo by Ross Stansfield

Company of Alexandria Light Infantry marching in Homecoming Parade, May 1909, on North Washington Street.

Courtesy of Laurence Fawcett

Chuck Beatley, Mayor of Alexandria from 1967 to July 1976, on top of City Hall. The familiar clock in the steeple on the Royal Street side is a landmark to all.

Photo by Ross Stansfield
Courtesy of ***Alexandria Port Packet***

The staff of the *Alexandria Port Packet,* Alexandria's newest newspaper, established March 25, 1975.

Staff photo courtesy of
Alexandria Port Packet

Young Alexandrian taking a break, 200 block South Pitt Street.

Photo by Ross Stansfield

The Christmas Walk is a ten year old early American celebration sponsored by the Alexandria Community Y. A fund raising project for the inner city welfare, the festival has emphasized the Scottish heritage for eight years. The photo shows Terry Wooten, R. J. Sweeney, Dez Calley, Bill Glasgow, Harland K. Heumann, and Kevin Thomson engaged in a pipe smoking contest in front of the Alexandria Pipe and Tobacco Company during the 1975 Christmas Walk.

Photo by Ross Stansfield

Scottish pipers march through the streets of Alexandria, adding color and music to the annual event.

Photo by Ross Stansfield

VOTE FOR THESE FIVE MEN
W. Albert Smoot
Robt. S. Jones
Arthur H. Bryant
Thos. J. Fannon
Ed. F. Ticer
THE CITIZENS' TICKET

The winning ticket of the first five councilmen to be elected under the "at large" plan. Mr. William A. Smoot was selected from the group to serve as mayor, taking office in September of 1922.

Courtesy of Anna Hill Stansfield

Early 1930s picture of District Judge Joseph C. Waddi in a high school play, wearing a straw hat.

Courtesy of Helen Day

Robert E. Singleterry, Alexandria painter and graphic artist, in front of his studio on 300 South Fairfax Street.

Photo by Ross Stansfield

Royal Barber Shop at 400 Wolfe Street. James Redd has been at this location for twenty-one years; he was previously at 401 Wolfe for thirteen years, and has been an Alexandrian barber for fifty years.

Photo by Ross Stansfield

The Reverend Norman Roberts in his fireman's uniform.

Courtesy of Charles Sampson

Frederick Tilp, architect and boating enthusiast.

Photo by Ross Stansfield

Eudora Lyles, community leader and winner of Outstanding Citizen Award and Woman of the Month citation in 1975.

Photo by Elsa Rosenthal

Connie Gray in Spanish-American uniform
around 1898.

Courtesy of John Gray

The face of the Confederate soldier.
Photo by Ross Stansfield

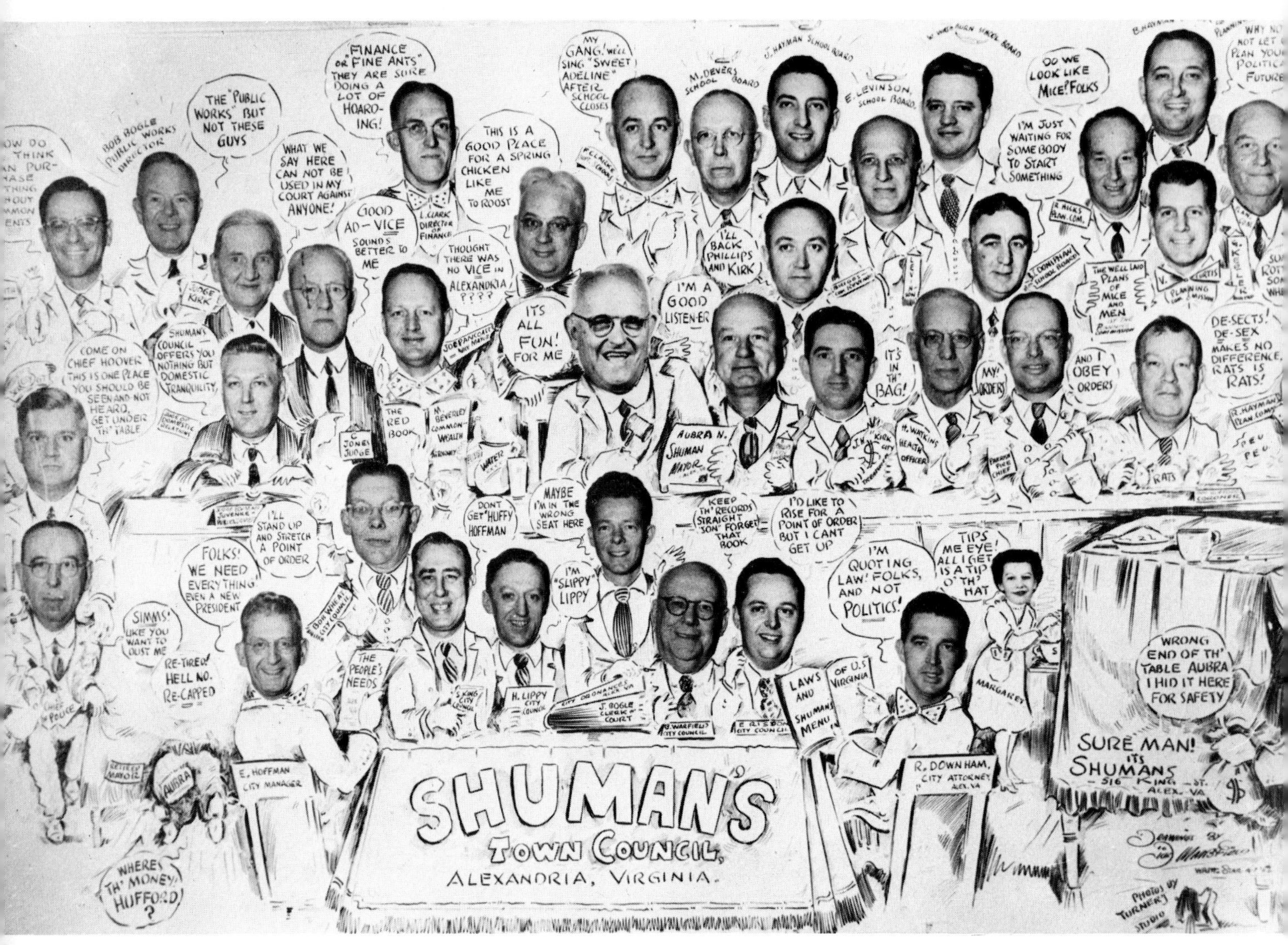

The faces of Alexandrians. This group "held council" in the mid-forties.

Courtesy of Charles Sampson

Mike Malone, Sonny Jurgensen, R. J. Sweeney, Dean McKnight.

Photo by Ross Stansfield

The third annual celebration of the Scottish Games held in July 1976 on the Episcopal High School campus. Sponsored by the Virginia Scottish Games Association, Incorporated, the games present an opportunity for all Scots and interested parties to gather for fun, festivity, and the perpetuation of Scottish culture.

Photos by Ross Stansfield

Faculty of the Alexandria County Schools in the late nineteenth century, left to right, are Annie Summers, Pearl Hoffman, Anna Schofield, Captain William H. Sweeny (a school superintendent), Colonel Theodore Ficklin, Alberta Sisson, Cora Webster Kelly, and Miss Thomas. Colonel Ficklin and Cora Kelly both have had schools named for them.

Courtesy of Edwina Warren

II. PLACES

Almost from its inception, Alexandria has held an impressive record of building and maintaining educational and religious facilities.

EDUCATION

From the time of the first grammar school housed in Town Hall to the numerous public and private schools of modern Alexandria, townspeople have worked to develop a sound educational system. The Alexandria Academy was the first free school in Northern Virginia. As early as 1785 Alexandrians recognized the need to educate all their children, not just those with ability to pay. The Academy followed the goals of public education that we attempt to achieve today. The Academy, along with the smaller Lancasterian School, remained the primary source of public education in Alexandria until 1830.

Education for girls was not ignored in Alexandria. Although the Academy definitely favored boys over girls when a choice was necessary, numerous schools and classes were available for young ladies. As early as 1797, a Miss May established such a school. Dr. James Muir conducted a girls' school, a venture taken over by his widow in 1820 and later his daughters. In 1812 a female free school opened on Columbus Street. This was endowed by Bartholomew Dandridge and run by Mrs. Fitz John Porter, who later initiated another on Washington and Prince Streets. In 1826 Ellen Mark began a forty-five year career of teaching little girls. Benjamin Hallowell educated the daughters of many townspeople, although it was his wife who at one point opened a school for girls in one room of the schoolhouse. Hallowell's nephew, James, operated a finishing school for girls for fifteen years prior to the Civil War. The education of the female population was not overlooked in Alexandria.

Around the turn of the century and into the early 1800s specialty schools were often advertised for men and women. Classes in needlework, dancing, and French abounded. A night school functioned at a cost of one dollar entrance fee and one dollar per month. For young children the popular "dame" schools were ever present. Of these, the best known was run by Mrs. Lucia Whiting and located on the second floor of the Star Engine House. General Fitzhugh Lee was among young students who attended there.

Probably the most popular school of the early nineteenth century was Hallowell's, which opened in 1824. Many Alexandria children received their education from this famous teacher. At about the same time, Mrs. Wilmer, widow of Dr. William Holland Wilmer, started a school for boys near the Theological Seminary. In 1837 a resolution was offered by J. P. B. Wilmer that a school be established under the care of the Episcopal church. Two years later the Episcopal High School located in Fairfax County just across the city line, began the education and training of the young men of Alexandria as well as those from distances away.

Also in the 1830s the Sisters of Charity opened a Catholic school for girls. This was short-lived, however, closing in 1840. At the same time, St. John's Academy for boys was forced to shut its doors for lack of supervision. In 1869 both St. Mary's Academy and St. Mary's Elementary School were formed, and have continued since that time.

A military school, also called St. John's Academy, was conducted by two brothers, William F. and Richard L. Carne. Boys of this school were often seen drilling in parade formation along the streets of the town. Before ending the venture in 1886, Richard L. Carne was appointed the first superintendent of Alexandria County schools. This occurred in January of 1871, the year which marked the beginning of the public education system.

As mandated by the law, public education was a dual system of segregated schools and would remain so for almost a century. Six schools were in operation the first year, four white and two black. Of the white schools, Washington and Curtis were the boys' institutions, Lee and Peabody for girls. Those for black children became known as Hallowell and Snowden, the latter for boys. Curtis and Peabody evidently merged with Washington and Lee respectively as the names of Curtis and Peabody were officially dropped by 1873. The Peabody name, however, remained more popular than Lee for years to come.

In 1908 the Lee School moved to a new location on Patrick and Prince Streets. That same year Theodore H. Ficklin began the first three year high school program in one room of the Washington Street School. A two year high school program for girls was started at Lee in 1909. By 1911 the program expanded to three years, and high school boys consolidated with high school girls of Lee School in the Prince Street building. Called the Alexandria High School, it occupied one wing of the building, graduating the first coeducational class in 1913. Lee School continued as a grammar school with grades one through seven, as did the Washington Street School.

The first four year high school program was instituted when the new Alexandria High School opened in 1915 on Cameron Street. At about this time West End School opened at the base of Shooter's Hill with first through fourth grades. School age population was growing, and by 1920 the need for a new black school was realized. Parker-Gray was built to accommodate elementary level boys and girls. It was named for the former principals of Hallowell and Snowden, Miss Sarah J. Gray, head of Hallowell from 1871 to 1892, and Mr. John F. Parker, Snowden's principal from 1875 to 1918.

Through annexation of land from Fairfax and Arlington Counties in 1930, Alexandria added three schools to its educational system. A three room black school was located in Mudtown, a community near the Theological Seminary. After that portion of Fairfax County was annexed to the city, the little school joined the school system, becoming known as Seminary School. Also obtained through annexation were the Mt. Vernon Elementary School and George Mason High School of

Alexandria High School around 1926. The building, located on Cameron and West, was razed for construction of the present Jefferson-Houston Elementary School.

Courtesy of George Washington High School

Erected in 1907, the old Mount Vernon Elementary School was razed after sixty years of service. The site, at 2601 Commonwealth Avenue, is now occupied by a new educational facility of the same name built in 1968.

Photo by Howard Olmsted, Jr.

Arlington County. In 1935 all of the Alexandria High School and George Mason High School students merged at the new George Washington High School on Mt. Vernon Avenue. This was the only white high school in Alexandria until the establishment of Francis C. Hammond High School in 1956.

In the 1930s the black enrollment grew significantly, and a new elementary school named Lyles-Crouch was started in the south end of town. For many years it was housed in an old silk factory until a new building was erected in 1958. The school took its name from two teachers of Hallowell and Snowden, Mr. Rosier Lyles and Mrs. Jane A. Crouch.

Also during the 1930s high school classes were started in Parker-Gray. Mr. Wesley D. Elam, then principal of Parker-Gray, was directly responsible for starting the program which saw its first graduates in 1936.

For a period of almost thirty years Mr. Thomas C. Williams was superintendent of the Alexandria Public Schools. Many significant changes came about during that time. Before the schools became integrated a new black school was opened in 1950 and acquired the

Arlington Institute in the 1890s. Located in the 200 block of South Washington Street, the school was run by Miss Chandlee for girls aged six through seventeen.

Courtesy of Anna Hill Stansfield

Parker-Gray name. The old Parker-Gray building was renamed Charles Houston for the prominent lawyer for the National Association for the Advancement of Colored People, who had fought for equalization of pay in the state school system. It became an elementary school for grades one through seven.

Alexandria's public schools are generally named for famous Americans or deserving Alexandrians. In addition to the previously named schools honoring Washington, Lee, and George Mason, educational facilities bear names of prominent citizens such as Adams, Tyler, Polk, Patrick Henry, and MacArthur. Theodore H. Ficklin School, named for the teacher, was in operation from 1949 to 1971. Also honoring a teacher was the Cora Kelly School (1955-1976). In existence today is the William Ramsay School as well a four schools named for Alexandrians of more recent distinction: Minnie Howard, Charles Barrett, Francis Hammond, and T. C. Williams.

Alexandria also has some excellent parochial schools. In addition to St. Mary's Academy and St. Mary's Elementary School, there are Ascension Academy for Catholic boys, incorporated in 1958, and Bishop Ireton, opened in 1964. The Episcopal High School has been in its location near the Theological Seminary since before the Civil War. St. Agnes Episcopal School for girls was established in 1925, with the school for boys, St. Stephen's, opening in 1944. All provide exceptional opportunities for students in the Alexandria area.

Potomac Academy classes of 1906 and 1907 before annexation of the town of Potomac.

Courtesy of Robert Howard

Prince Street School (1000 Block) in 1913. This class of 1916 includes Laurence Fawcett, Earl Sullivan, Francis Nugent, Edwin Graham and Peter Pulman.

Courtesy of Laurence Fawcett

Fifth grade class at Lee School in 1913.

Courtesy of Charles Sampson

Girls' basketball team, Alexandria High School in 1927.

Courtesy of George Washington High School

Jefferson School in 1923. Second from left is Cora Webster Kelly; also included are school nurse Mary Monroe, second row, right, and Margaret Abramson, first row, second on left.

Courtesy of Charles Sampson

Thomas Champlin Williams, Superintendent of Schools from 1933 to 1961.

Courtesy of George Washington High School

Parker-Gray in 1920.

Courtesy of Helen Day

Football team with Mr. Ferris Holland, left, a science teacher responsible for starting many of Parker-Gray's athletic endeavors, and Wesley D. Elam, right, a leading force in establishing Parker-Gray as an accredited high school.

Courtesy of Helen Day

Parker-Gray class of 1947. In center front is Nelly Brooks Quanda, seated, fourth from left, and on her right, Miss Christine Howard. Both became principals of Jefferson-Houston School.

Courtesy of Helen Day

Science and home economics classes at Parker-Gray 1946 or 1947.

Courtesy of Helen Day

Patrick H. Lumpkins taught in Snowden School for thirty-nine years. He and his daughter Helen Day have combined teaching years totaling eighty-five.

Courtesy of Helen Day

Convent of St. Mary's Academy grounds, 2404 Russell Road. This house was once owned by a member of the Alexander family. The school moved here from the Prince Street location in 1943. A large brick building occupies the area in front of the convent.

Courtesy of St. Mary's Academy

The St. Agnes Spring Fair in 1976. This was the original school building on Fontain Street.

Photo by Ross Stansfield

St. Mary's basketball team in 1935.

Courtesy of St. Mary's Academy

May Day ceremony at St. Mary's Academy, 1952.

Courtesy of St. Mary's Academy

Mrs. Mini-Haha Stansbury Howard (1868-1950), a community leader interested in day care and recreational centers for children. She was instrumental in obtaining Quaker burial grounds (current site of library) for a playground. An elementary school is named for her.

Courtesy of Evelyn Hunter

Lillian Holland, assistant Principal of Lyles-Crouch for eight years, was in the Alexandria school system for forty-three years (one year in Fairfax). She was also the only woman and black on the Fair Housing Board organized in 1969.

Courtesy of Lillian Holland

George Washington High School Junior Class of 1950.

Courtesy of George Washington High School

Top—left: Over the top. *Right:* What a play!
Bottom—left: 'Ray for our side! *Right:* Carow on the Rampage.

The President of the United States attends a college football game at our own G. W. stadium.

Hoxton Hall, the oldest building on the Episcopal High School campus, is named for Archibald Robinson Hoxton, Sr., head master from 1931 to 1947. Previously used both for classes and as a home, the building now houses the administrative offices.

Courtesy of Episcopal High School

Francis C. Hammond, killed in action on March 27, 1953, in Korea, was posthumously awarded the Congressional Medal of Honor for gallantry. A school named in his honor was dedicated in 1956. Francis C. Hammond Junior High is located at 2646 Seminary Road.

Courtesy of Francis C. Hammond High School

T. C. Williams High School rowing team and group in front of school on King Street.

Courtesy of T. C. Williams High School

Mr. Robert A. (Tony) Hanley, Principal of T. C. Williams High School since 1972, and students.

Photo by Ross Stansfield

RELIGION

The first two churches in Alexandria began serving the community within a year of each other, Christ Episcopal Church in 1773 and the Presbyterian Church the following year. Both have remained active and important parts of Alexandria ever since.

Christ Church grew from a division of the Truro Parish in 1765. The new Fairfax Parish contracted to build a church in Alexandria almost immediately. The building, known as the "Church in the Woods" or "The Church nigh Alexandria," was not completed until 1773. Outside the town limits, it often was difficult to reach when muddy roads became impassable. George Washington owned a pew and regularly attended church when he was in town. His memorial service, however, was held in the Presbyterian Meeting House since the "Church in the Woods" was practically inaccessible at the time.

For more than two hundred years Christ Church has managed to keep its doors open for all those who wish to worship there. Neither fire, war, nor lack of leadership have forced it to close for a lengthy period of time. It is a church rich in tradition and heritage with many names associated with the growth of the town listed in its records. The Washington, Fairfax, Mason, Lee, and Curtis families worshiped there, and John Dalton, James Wren, and John Alexander are names linked with the history of the church.

The church has been served by distinguished members of the clergy. A son of William Fairfax, Bryan, was rector for a time. He succeeded the Reverend David Griffith, a close friend of Washington who filled the positions of both physician and minister during the Revolutionary War years. The Reverend Charles B. Dana baptised and confirmed children of both the Curtis and Lee families, including Robert E. Lee, who attended the church throughout his boyhood and was confirmed there in 1853. The Reverend William Meade officiated only two years, but the Virginia Bishop is well remembered by Alexandrians for his association with the church.

It is customary for the President of the United States to visit Christ Church on the Sunday nearest George Washington's Birthday sometime during his term in office. Presidents Wilson and Roosevelt brought with them the current Prime Ministers of England, David Lloyd George and Winston Churchill.

It is interesting to note that the construction of Christ Church, then part of the Established Church of England, was completed

The Reverend William Sydnor in front of pulpit in Christ Church.

Photo by Ben T. Boogher, Jr.

Christ Church, 118 North Washington Street. Inset shows monument to Charles Bennett, a bachelor who willed his estate to the city of Alexandria. In appreciation, Benjamin Latrobe was hired to design the monument in his honor.

Photo by Ross Stansfield

by John Carlyle, a Scotsman and a Presbyterian. Carlyle received the commission to finish the church in 1772 when James Parsons failed to meet his contract. About that same time, Carlyle began planning a building for his own Presbyterian congregation, which was meeting in an upper room of Town Hall. With the project underway, the Reverend William Thom answered the call of the congregation and would have served in the new building had it not been for his untimely death in August of 1773. For several years members of the congregation took turns leading the services. In 1780, the Reverend Isaac Keith arrived. He remained with the church for eight years and was followed in 1789 by Scottish Reverend Dr. James Muir, who served the church until his death thirty-one years later. He was a well known figure in the community, acting as a chaplain in the Masonic lodge, as a trustee of the Alexandria Academy, and President of the Alexandria Library Company. By his own wish, the grave of this much respected and well loved individual now lies in front of the pulpit of the church that he served so well.

Tragedy struck in 1835 when fire all but destroyed the structure of the Presbyterian Church. Although much of the interior wood, glass, and even the organ was saved, it took two years to rebuild the structure. Dr. Elias Harrison, minister at the time of destruction, lived to witness harder years during the Civil War period. In 1865, two years after Harrison's death, the congregation was listed as sixty-five. In 1899 the second Presbyterian Church took title to the property, and for fifty years the church was closed. The congregation reactivated in 1949 as the Old Presbyterian Meeting House and is prospering today.

Two Alexandria churches developed as a result of congregational dissension within the membership. In 1809 the Reverend William Gibson resigned as rector of Christ Church, taking with him a portion of the congregation faithful to his beliefs. The group purchased a small wooden building on Fairfax Street, and a vestry of the new St. Paul's Episcopal Church was organized in January of 1810. Reverend Gibson remained with the church for one year, to be succeeded by the Reverend William Wilmer. As rector for fourteen years, Reverend Wilmer contributed much to the community as well as to his church. He helped found the Theological Seminary, assisted with organization of a church in the District of Columbia, worked with the rector of Christ Church to develop various religious programs, and started educational and religious activities within St. Paul's. By 1817 the congregation had outgrown the little wooden building, and the present

The Presbyterian Meeting House, 321 South Fairfax Street. The steeple was placed at the rear of the church after reconstruction in the 1830s. In the historic graveyard are buried Dr. James Craik, Brigadier General Lewis Nicola, John Carlyle, and William Hunter, founder of St. Andrew Society. Inset shows the church from the front.

Photo by Ross Stansfield
Inset Courtesy of Alexandria Tourist Council

structure was erected. Designed by Benjamin Latrobe, St. Paul's became an Alexandria landmark. Additions and architectural changes have enhanced its elegance.

As the people of St. Paul's prepared to move from the chapel on Fairfax Street, members of the congregation of the First Presbyterian Church were disagreeing on an issue that caused a split within their ranks. The seceding members left the church, purchased the little wooden chapel, and formed the Second Presbyterian Church. They remained in that location for some years until a new building was erected on the corner of St. Asaph and Prince Streets.

The colorful beginning of the Baptist church in Northern Virginia is familiar. Jeremiah Moore was an itinerant preacher who at the age of twenty-six received his calling to go and preach the gospel throughout the countryside. At that time, the Established Church of England was by law the only religious organization permitted, although the Act of Tolerance did grant some concessions to groups such as the Presbyterians. Moore refused to comply with the law and was arrested and jailed in Alexandria. Through the bars of the jailhouse Moore continued to preach to the gathering crowds. The question of religious tolerance was justified, and Moore was soon permitted to preach the gospel as he desired. By the end of the Revolution he had formed a Baptist church in Backlick, Virginia. In 1803 members of this congregation formed the Alexandria Baptist Society and erected a building on Washington Street. Moore was among the itinerant preachers who served in this church during its beginning years. The original structure was destroyed by fire in 1829, but was rebuilt on the same site. By 1926 First Baptist could boast of having the largest congregation in town. The growing membership moved to a new location on King Street in 1954, selling the old building to another Baptist group. The congregation of Downtown Baptist has preserved the historic structure and maintained Baptist ministry in the Old Town area.

Methodism began with the formation of the Society in Alexandria in 1774. Young Reverend

The Reverend Dr. James Muir of Presbyterian Meeting House from 1789 to 1820.
Courtesy of Presbyterian Meeting House

Old sketch of First Presbyterian Church before the fire of 1835. In 1929 the church took its current name of Old Presbyterian Meeting House.

Courtesy of Clement Conger

We Hold These Truths by George Klop, presented in the Presbyterian Meeting House.

Photo by Ross Stansfield
Courtesy of ***Alexandria Port Packet***

Sketch of a home, 323 South Fairfax Street, alongside the Meeting House. This Federal period building, wrongly attributed to Colonel George Deneale, was a vacant lot until 1840 (after the fire). It was built by Charles B. Unruh in the mid-forties.

Courtesy of Jean Elliot

William Duke led the group of twelve believers which included another dedicated seventeen-year-old, John Littlejohn. As the Society grew, Francis Asbury, sent to America by John Wesley, made frequent missionary visits to the town. He often preached in Market Square or sometimes used the Presbyterian Church. Appointed in 1791, Ezekial Cooper became the first minister of the Alexandria Station of the Methodist Episcopal Church holding services in the meeting house in Chapel Alley off Duke Street. While visiting in 1804, Francis Asbury dedicated a new building located on Washington Street between Prince and King Streets. A group left this congregation in 1829 to form a Methodist Protestant denomination in a church near King and Washington Streets.

When Methodism split over slavery, the Southern faction organized the Washington Street Methodist Church. Built in 1849, the structure was directly across from that of the Northern Methodists, who, in 1883, took the name Trinity Methodist. The Northern and Southern factions became nationally unified in 1939, and three years later the old Trinity Methodist Church was razed and a new structure erected at 2911 Cameron Mills Road. The Washington Street Methodist, now a United Methodist Church, exists in its original location.

The Catholic church of Alexandria owes its

The Reverend Leon Laylor, Rector of St. Paul's Church 1958 to 1971.

Courtesy of St. Paul's Church

St. Paul's Episcopal Church on Pitt and Duke Streets shown around 1906 and in a current photo. This structure was designed by architect Benjamin Latrobe, whose work includes the South Wing of the nation's Capitol and the Roman Catholic Cathedral in Baltimore, Maryland.

Courtesy of Laurence Fawcett

Downtown Baptist Church, 212 South Washington Street.

Photo by Charlie Brown

St. Mary's Catholic Church, 310 Duke Street.

Courtesy of Charles Sampson

Woodcut of Washington Street Temple Beth El, occupied from 1871 to 1955.

Courtesy of Beth El Temple

The religious school, shown here in 1945, outgrew temple facilities by 1950, using a public school until the new temple was available. Classes in Judaism range from nursery level to confirmation at age fifteen or sixteen for over 350 students.

Courtesy of Beth El Temple

beginning to Colonel John Fitzgerald for his dedication and tenacity, and to Robert Hooe for his generosity. In the late 1700s these two men met in Fitzgerald's home and discussed the possibility of starting a church. General Washington supported the project, and Fitzgerald began the task of collecting subscriptions for the church while Hooe arranged the donation of land for both a church and graveyard. Not until 1785 was the Act Establishing Religious Freedom passed; therefore, Catholic worshipers were restricted in their activities until that time. By 1795, with religious freedom a reality, a brick chapel was built on the land donated by Hooe at the southern end of Washington Street, the present site of St. Mary's cemetery. When the building was razed in 1810 the congregation moved to the former Methodist meeting house on Chapel Alley. The present building on Duke Street was erected in 1826 back to back with the chapel that had served more than one denomination.

Over the years St. Mary's Parish has maintained not only the church but also excellent educational facilities. A mission church, St. Rita's, was established in 1913. Becoming a separate parish in 1924, St. Rita's now maintains a church and school on Russell Road.

The history of the Jewish population in Alexandria begins in the 1850s with the migration of German Hebrews from Prussia. In 1857 the Hebrew Benevolent Society was organized in order to arrange for appropriate burial grounds for the Jewish community. Formation of a congregation followed. Named Beth El, it is the oldest Reform Jewish congregation in Northern Virginia and the second oldest in the Commonwealth. In 1871 the Beth El congregation moved into a temple on Washington Street north of Christ Church. For years the congregation had no rabbi; however, in 1939, Rabbi Hugo Schiff arrived from Germany, literally rescued from a concentration camp. Except for one year the expanding congregation has since maintained spiritual leadership. From 1957 they have worshiped in a contemporary two-story temple on Seminary Road.

Agudas Achim is the Conservative Jewish Synagogue serving Northern Virginia. Established on Wolfe Street in 1914, the temple moved to Russell Road before locating on Valley Drive in 1958. A branch religious school operates from Ravensworth Baptist Church in Annandale.

Alfred Street Baptist, 313 South Alfred Street.
Photo by Ron Colbroth

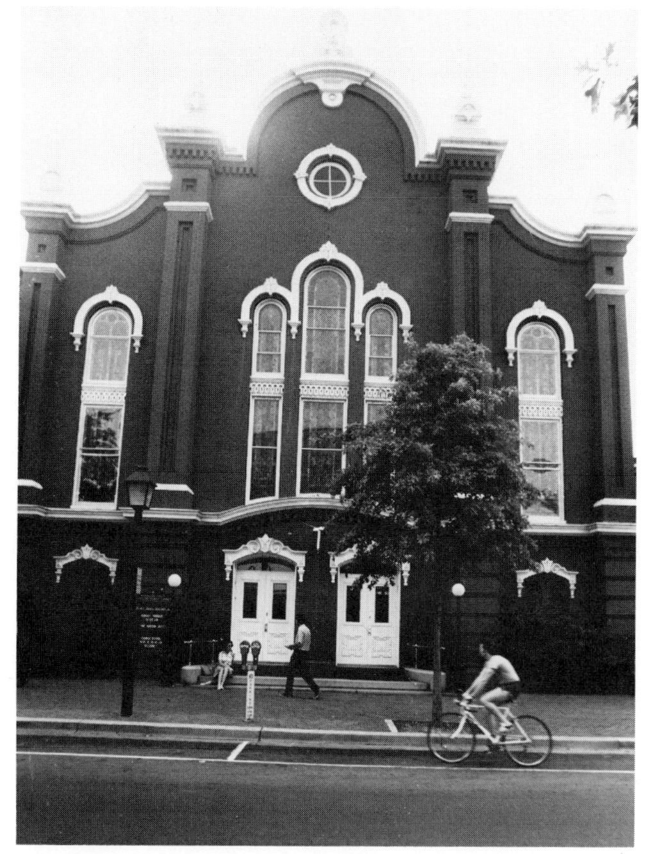

Washington Street Methodist, 115 South Washington Street.

Photo by Ross Stansfield

Free Methodist Church, 201 Prince Street, once the Old Dominion Bank, now the Athenaeum, home of the Northern Virginia Fine Arts Association since 1964.

Courtesy of Alexandria Library

Jackquelin Strange (1837-1923), Pastor at Roberts Chapel.

Courtesy of John Gray

First Christian Church, 2723 King Street.
Photo by Ross Stansfield

Church of Jesus Christ of Latter Day Saints, 2810 King Street.
Photo by Ross Stansfield

Church of God, 2912 King Street.
Photo by Ross Stansfield

First Baptist Church, 2932 King Street.

Photo by Ross Stansfield

Oakland Baptist Church, 3408 King Street.

Photo by Ross Stansfield

Fairlington Presbyterian Church, 3846 King Street.

Photo by Ross Stansfield

Fairlington United Methodist Church, 3900 King Street.

Photo by Ross Stansfield

THEOLOGICAL SEMINARY

The Protestant Episcopal Theological Seminary is second oldest and one of the largest theological seminaries of the Episcopal Church. In 1815 the Diocese of Virginia resolved to establish a training center for clergy, giving rise to the Educational Society of Maryland and Virginia. Formed in 1818, the society included Francis Scott Key as one of its lay members. The Reverend William H. Wilmer, as president, is credited as a founder of the seminary.

The Seminary celebrates its beginning as 1823, when Wilmer taught in his study at St. Paul's and Dr. Reuel Keith conducted classes in temporary quarters on King and Washington Streets. The Reverend Oliver Norris, Rector of Christ Church, became a professor in 1825. By 1827 the Seminary moved to its present location off Seminary Road in northwest Alexandria.

The Seminary offers a three-year Master in Divinity program as well as a two-year Master in Theological Studies and a Doctor of Ministry degree. Its enrollment of over two hundred includes foreign students and women preparing for ordination. It emphasizes both parish ministry and overseas missions.

The Reverend William H. Wilmer, Rector of St. Paul's Episcopal Church from 1812 to 1826.

Courtesy St. Paul's Church

The Protestant Episcopal Seminary. Tower on Aspinwall was given by Chinese Christians as a thank offering for missionaries from the Seminary.

Photo by Ben T. Boogher, Jr.

ALEXANDRIA ACADEMY

This small building on Washington Street used the Lancasterian Method of teaching, therefore was known as Lancasterian School. Note the Alexandria Academy to the rear.

Courtesy of Alexandria Library

The Alexandria Academy was a private pay school when a group of citizens approached George Washington with a request for assistance in establishing a fund for education of the poor. Washington's concern for public education was evident from the numerous contributions he made to educational institutions. He aided the Academy by paying fifty pounds annually and by bequeathing it approximately four thousand dollars.

Chartered by the Virginia General Assembly in 1786, its cornerstone had been laid the previous year. In 1812 the small Lancasterian School was built beside the Academy to accommodate additional pupils. Both schools were under the supervision of the Academy trustees.

By 1816 the Academy began having financial problems, and from 1824 to 1835 it was closed from time to time. In 1853 Edward Powell bought it, but it became the property of the School Board in 1884 when the current owner died.

The original cornerstone of the building was discovered in 1928 beneath the basement floor of the Academy. Four years later, a ceremony was held to install a plaque on the building with the date that marked its beginning and the names of the first Board of Trustees.

Alexandria Academy in 1929.

Courtesy of National Archives

Washington Street School in 1929. Erected in 1882 on the site of the Lancasterian School, the building was converted into administrative offices for the public school system in 1953.

Courtesy of National Archives

Present administrative offices of the public school system, formerly the Washington Street School. Academy is shown on the left.

Photo by Ross Stansfield

ALIVE (Alexandrians Involved Ecumenically) day care center in 1976.

Photo by Ross Stansfield

COMMUNITY Y

The Alexandria Community Y occupies two houses in the historic Old Town portion of the city. The flounder section of one of the buildings is believed to have been built by James Parson in the late 1700s. At various times the house was used as a guest house for Gadsby's tavern and for a while as a boarding house run by Mrs. Polly Washington. In the 1940s the home was sold to the new YWCA organization by Frances Parkinson Keyes. During World War II it became a residence for girls, but soon expanded services to programs of youth activities and continued education. In the 1950s the YWCA opened a second center on Alfred Street. After a time it was realized that the center was not meeting community needs, but instead stood as a misinterpreted symbol of segregation. The Alfred Street center was closed, and programs continued in the present Y building.

In 1963 the Alexandria YWCA became part of the National Capital Area organization. It remained under this system ten years, but found that difficulties in working with the larger structure outweighed advantages. In order to get back in touch with this city the center left the national organization to become an autonomous community project not affiliated with the YWCA. Its programs involve numerous educational opportunities: a Head Start program, Project Pulse Point, Thanksgiving food baskets, city tours, and various fund raising events such as the Scottish Christmas Walk. It responds to the needs of the community as well as offering many benefits to the women of Alexandria.

Mrs. Elizabeth Ann Compagna, left, director of Alexandria Y.

Courtesy of Alexandria Y

Tour docents at Christ Church.
Courtesy of Alexandria Y

Head Start students in 1975.
Courtesy of Alexandria Y

HOPKINS HOUSE

Hopkins House has been filling a community need since it opened its doors on Gibbon Street in 1939. Originally instituted as an off-shoot of a day nursery, Hopkins House rapidly expanded to include as many community activities as interested citizens could provide. Its name reflects an ideal of dedicated service. Dr. J. Milton Hopkins was loved and respected by the numerous families he attended. The spirit of his caring is projected daily through the traditions of Hopkins House.

The list of activities now in effect range from pre-school programs through senior citizen services. School age children can benefit from private tutoring, summer camp, recreational groups, clubs, and work shops. Vocational, educational, and career counseling is available. A program for the Spanish speaking community is included as well as groups active in initiating social change. Of utmost importance is the emergency relief that Hopkins House provides for those in need of food, clothes, or shelter. The list continues as Hopkins House grows along with the people it serves.

Old Hopkins House, 1312 Princess Street.
Courtesy of Hopkins House

Connie Chissell, first director of Hopkins House.
Courtesy of Hopkins House

Dance group in the fifties.
Courtesy of Hopkins House

Ground breaking for new building, March 24, 1974.

Courtesy of Hopkins House

New building, 1224 Princess Street.

Photo by Ross Stansfield

ALEXANDRIA LIBRARY

The library, as a public institution, was established in 1937 when Dr. Robert South Barrett gave funds to construct the current building in honor of his Mother, Kate Waller Barrett. At the same time the Society of Friends granted a ninety-nine year lease for use of land which had been the Quaker burial grounds. The City Council added the library's operating expenses to its budget, and the Library Company contributed its book collection and funds for equipping the library.

As a subscription library, the establishment dates back to 1794. At that time the Alexandria Library Company was formed with James Muir as president and Edward Stabler as secretary and treasurer. In 1798 the Virginia Assembly granted an Act of Incorporation to the Company. An active part of the public library, it supplies three members to the seven member board. Presentation of an annual lecture was resumed in 1957, preserving its historic and cultural role within the community.

The original library building operates on Queen Street, although the contents of the Virginiana and Alexandriana Rooms, as well as manuscripts and archival materials, have been moved to the historic Lloyd House on the corner of Washington and Queen Streets. Two branches have been opened in other parts of the city, the Ellen Coolidge Burke on Seminary Road and the James M. Duncan, Jr., in Del Ray.

The Lloyd House, 220 North Washington Street, has been renovated for use by the public library. In it are housed the rare book collection of the Alexandria Library Company as well as reference material from the Virginiana Room of the Queen Street building. Built in 1797 by John Wise, the structure exemplifies the fine Georgian architecture of this city. It was occupied by such notables as James Marshall, brother of Supreme Court Chief Justice John Marshall, and Jacob Hoffman, an Alexandria mayor. Mrs. James Hooe was landlady to schoolmaster Benjamin Hallowell who used the home as both residence and classroom.

John Lloyd and wife, Anne Harriotte Lee, were owners from 1832 until 1918 when the home passed into the hands of the Smoot family. After serving as a rooming house during World War II, the house stood empty, facing destruction. It was saved from demolition in 1968 and restored for its present use in 1976.

Photo by Ron Colbroth

Public Library building, 717 Queen Street.

Photo by Ron Colbroth

MASONIC MEMORIAL

The Alexandria-Washington Lodge number 22 had its beginnings in 1782 when a petition was sent to Pennsylvania asking for permission to open a Lodge at Alexandria. The Alexandria Lodge number 39 was organized the following year and continued until 1786, when it changed its charter to the Grand Lodge at Richmond, Virginia. At this time the registry number became 22, and George Washington was elected the first Master of the Lodge. After his death, the Washington name was added in honor of the Brother Mason.

Alexandria Masons often participate in significant ceremonies in Virginia and the District of Columbia. In 1785 they laid the cornerstone of the Alexandria Academy and six years later assisted in the ceremonial placing of the cornerstone of the District of Columbia at Jones Point. They helped lay the cornerstone of the United States Capitol in 1793. When General Lafayette visited the United States in 1824, the Alexandria-Washington Lodge saw that he was properly entertained. The Lodge also assisted in the funeral service of the seven firemen who lost their lives in an Alexandria fire in 1855. Throughout the years, the Lodge continued to grow and work within the community. Its charities are numerous as the brotherhood helps where needed.

The most prominent structure in Alexandria is the towering monument erected by the Masonic Fraternity of the United States to honor George Washington and to preserve relics that were in the possession of Lodge number 22. Plans for the monument began at a meeting here in 1910. On May 12, 1932, the building was dedicated in a momentous ceremony attended by President Herbert Hoover. The ground floor contains the Assembly Room, Shrine Museum, dining room, and kitchen. Above this is Memorial Hall, Lodge Room, Replica Lodge Room, and North Room. The seven levels of the Tower house the museum, library, Grotto Archives, Cryptic Room, Chapel, and Observation Platform. The temple and all the items contained within the handsome structure remind visitors of the first President's high ideals and pay tribute to him as a Mason.

Thomas Andrew Hulfish, Jr., at Shooter's Hill around 1908 or 1909.

Courtesy of Mrs. Thomas Hulfish

The employees who constructed the Masonic Temple around 1923.

Courtesy of Peggy Kleysteuber

Masonic group in front of Southern Railway Office, 906 Prince Street, taken in 1923 when the Masonic Memorial was dedicated.

Courtesy of Charles Sampson

A 1931 photo of the Masonic Memorial on Shooter's Hill, viewed from the east. Note that the correct spelling is "Shooter," not Shuter as is often written. The knoll is named for a hill near London, England, from which "shooters" hunted.

Courtesy of National Archives

George R. Hill in Knight's Temple uniform.
Courtesy of Anna Hill Stansfield

Businessman and Mason of Alexandria, George R. Hill in ceremonial robes, circa 1900.
Courtesy of Anna Hill Stansfield

Photo by Ross Stansfield

Catt's Tavern on King's Highway was frequented by drovers. Slave trading was held there annually on January 1.

Courtesy of Mrs. Thomas Hulfish

TAVERNS

In colonial days taverns had particular significance in the lives of townspeople as well as travelers. A tavern was a place where weary adventurers could rest for a night and eat a good meal served by a kindly host. It was also a place for the townsfolk to meet when important issues had to be discussed or future plans determined. And, just as important, it could be a place for social life and entertainment.

The best known of all the taverns in Alexandria is Gadsby's or Mason's Ordinary as it was originally called. John Gadsby was never an owner of the tavern, but as manager and host he created an inn that was famous beyond the continent and still maintains its charm. The tavern consists of two buildings. The older portion was built in 1752 and was owned by Charles and Ann Mason. For fifteen years after the death of Ann Mason in 1761, the Ordinary was under the management of John Carlyle. Known over the years as the City Tavern, the Coffee House, the Fountain, the Bunch of Grapes, and probably other colorful long-forgotten names, the hostelry entered its golden years under the ownership of John Wise, who purchased the small building in 1782. The larger structure was erected by him in 1792, and soon after, John Gadsby became official innkeeper. Gadsby called the inn the City Tavern and Hotel. His twelve years as proprietor saw numerous historic events and social gatherings. The beautiful ballroom with its suspended musicians' balcony has been the site of many brilliant affairs including several Washington Birthnight Balls. Despite the long list of managers, the inn has maintained the popular Gadsby name.

Other taverns flourished in Alexandria at the time of Gadsby's fame. McKnight's was also frequented by Washington and was used at least once by the St. Andrew's Society for a St. John's Day banquet. The Rainbow Inn could be easily found in its day by a colorful arch over the portal. The popular Royal George or "George" was known for dancing and entertainment. It operated until 1857 when the old building was torn down. There were few houses on the western side of Washington Street when the Washington Tavern operated in the late 1700s. The building stayed in its location at the intersection of King and Washington until 1879. Also bearing the Washington name was a tavern on King and Pitt Streets. In its early years it proudly displayed the sign of General Washington on Horseback. Later it was better known by another name, the Marshall House, scene of bloodshed at the start of the Civil War.

Other taverns bore quaint names such as Red Lion, Lamb's Tavern, and Indian Queen. There is no doubt that Alexandria had its share of gathering places where one could eat and talk and perhaps sip wine or ale with a friend. These hostelries were famous for excellent accommodations as well as social ambience.

On the corner of King and Peyton Streets, The Old Virginia House later became known as Jackson's Hotel. A tornado demolished it in 1927.

Courtesy of Mrs. Thomas Hulfish

City Hotel, left photo, around 1910. The smaller building, photographed in 1924, is located to the left of the hotel. Together they are known as Gadsby's and are situated on Royal and Cameron Streets.

Courtesy of National Archives

Horatio Clagett (1777-1844), painted by James Eaches. Clagett came to Alexandria from Port Tobacco, Maryland, and became innkeeper of The Sign of General Washington on Horseback. He was the proprietor of Gadsby's, called Clagett's Hotel, in 1824 officiating at two momentous occasions: the Washington Birthnight Ball which included Vice President Daniel D. Tompkins and Henry Clay, and an October banquet for Lafayette with John Quincy Adams as one of the guests.

Courtesy of Mrs. Thomas L. Wattles

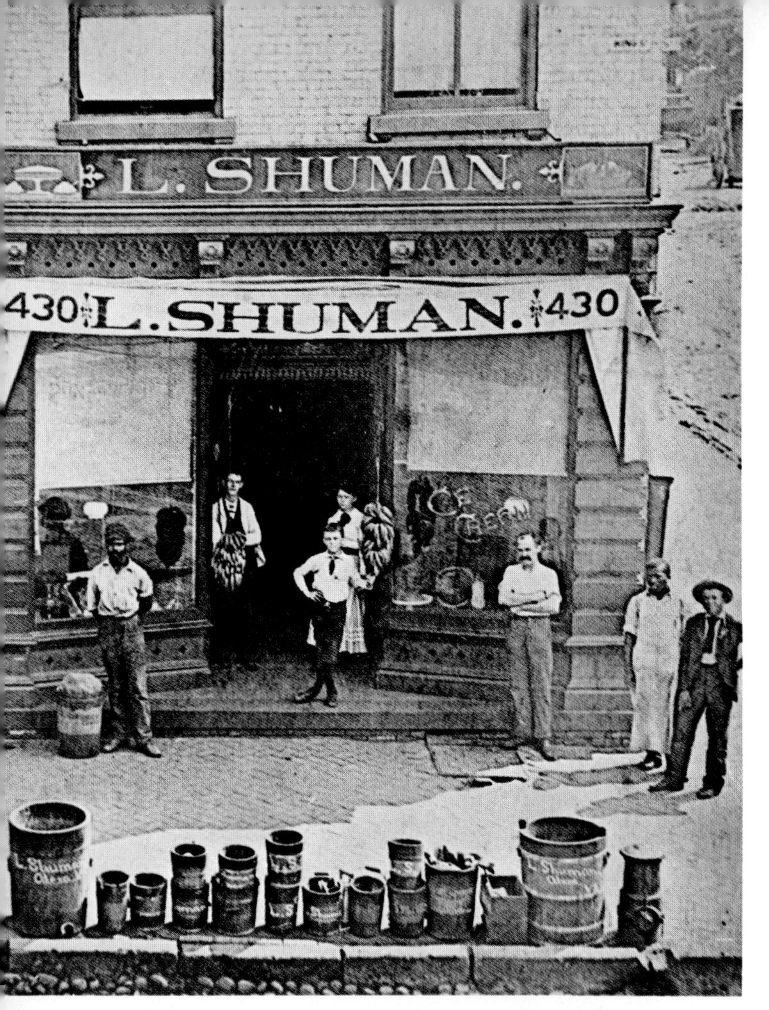

Shuman's moved to Marshall House in 1884 although this location was temporary.

Courtesy of Shuman's Bakery

SHUMAN'S BAKERY

Jelly cake from Shuman's Bakery is an item so renowned that even Queen Elizabeth II has sampled it. As the Queen (then Princess) and Prince Philip were preparing to return to England in 1951, an order for hard rolls and jelly cake was placed with Shuman's for the royal couple to take with them. Many Alexandrians will agree that Shuman's is worthy of its international fame.

The Shuman family history dates back to 1825 when Johannes Ernest Shuman came to Alexandria from Germany. His son, Louis Philip, opened a bakery and ice cream business toward the end of the century. In 1892, Louis' nephew, Aubra Newton Shuman, came to live with Louis and began work in the shop. Soon he became a master baker and opened his own bakery in another city. Upon the death of Louis P. Shuman, Aubra returned to Alexandria and became owner of the business. Following in the Shuman tradition, the bakery passed from Aubra to his son-in-law, Irvin M. Hufford, husband of Frances Shuman. The present owner, Avalon Blackburn Marchant III, is the son of Virginia Shuman Marchant, thus maintaining the Shuman family ties with the famous bakery now located at 430 South Washington Street.

The Shuman family.

Courtesy of Shuman's Bakery

Shuman's Bakery on King Street. Pictured with the oxcart are Mrs. Sandeel and her daughter, Catherine, who visited once a week from Prince William County to sell produce.

Courtesy of Shuman's Bakery

Kretol Chemical Company around 1900.
Courtesy of Alexandria Library

Captains Row, 100 block of Prince Street.
Courtesy of Alexandria Tourist Council

Painting of warehouse on Union Street where
Dockside Sales is now located.

Courtesy of Robert G. Whitton

An outing at Hume Springs around 1900.
Courtesy of Anna Hill Stansfield

In 1965 the Department of Planning and Community Development began an ambitious face-lifting project for Old Town Alexandria. Restoration and reconstruction continue today as efforts are made to preserve and maintain the historic structures of the city. The following photos exemplify the process of change over the years.

Downtown Alexandria during urban renewal.

Courtesy of Department of Planning and Community Development

The 400 block of King Street before urban renewal.

Courtesy of Department of Planning and Community Development

A view of the King and Pitt Street intersection after reconstruction.

Photo by Ross Stansfield

Alexandria National Bank before urban renewal.

Courtesy of Department of Planning and Community Development

Current photo of Alexandria National Bank with City Hall and Market Square in the background.

Photo by Ross Stansfield

Downtown Alexandria photographed from City Hall rooftop before urban renewal.

Courtesy of Department of Planning and Community Development

In order to avoid destruction, this old home was moved from an area undergoing reconstruction. The photo, taken in the fall of 1975, shows the move down King Street to a new location on South Pitt.

Photo by Ross Stansfield

Ceremony at reconstructed Carlyle House with the First Virginia Regiment demonstrating colonial manual of arms, April 1976.

Photo by Ross Stansfield

Market Square under urban renewal in 1968.

Courtesy of Department of Planning and Community Development

Courtesy of Michael and Michael Architects

This charming little home in Ross Alley is the renovated ice house of William and Craig Hudnall. The photo above shows the structure in its original state.

Photo by Ross Stansfield

The fountain's majestic spray is shown in this 1976 photo of Market Square and City Hall. Although it has undergone numerous changes, the Square occupies the same space originally chosen before the 1749 auctions. City Hall, built in 1873, and Market Square share a block bordered by King and Cameron Streets and North Fairfax and North Royal.

Photo by Ross Stansfield
Courtesy of Alexandria Port Packet

Fashion designer Frankie Welch stands before her shop at 305 Cameron Street. Popularly known as the Duvall House, the building was once a tavern where George Washington was entertained. Lawyer and Attorney General Charles Lee rented from William Duvall from 1788 to 1790. Shortly after, the structure housed the Bank of Alexandria until the completion of the bank building on the southeast corner of North Fairfax and Cameron Streets.

Photo by Ross Stansfield

Henry Hobbs of the Christmas Attic. The structure that houses his shop was once one of the many waterfront warehouses.

Photo by Ross Stansfield

Peggy Kleysteuber and Maya of the Cash Grocer Health Food Store, located at 1313 King Street.

Photo by Ross Stansfield
Courtesy of ***Alexandria Port Packet***

Peter C. Montague's ancestors owned a dry goods store and ship chandler's store on the same block. He now owns a clog shop at 203 King Street.

Photo by Ross Stansfield

This house, which was located on Daingerfield Island north of the Alexandria business district, was of the type frequently used by rumrunners, gamblers, and ladies of the evening.

Courtesy of Frederick Tilp

The Chequire House, built in 1797 by Bernard Chequire. The bottom floor was used as a shop and the rest of the house was a residence. This building now houses the Market Square Shop and is one of the few remaining houses which has dual usage by the store owner as a shop and residence.

Photo by Ross Stansfield

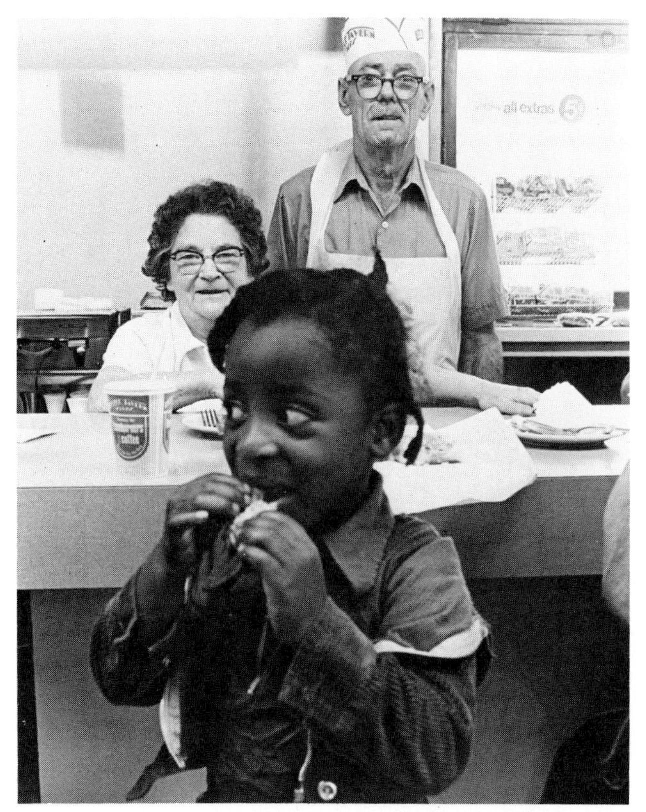

The Little Tavern at 828 North Washington Street.

Photo by Ross Stansfield
Courtesy of ***Alexandria Port Packet***

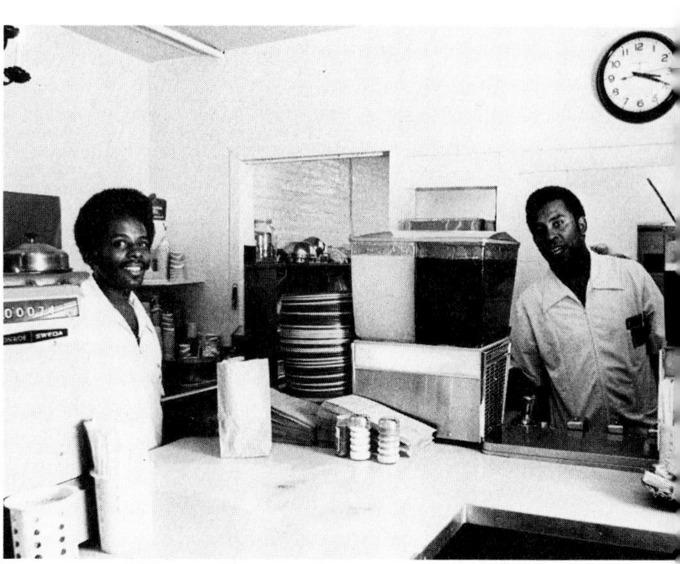

Leroy and Tony Gee of the Snack Bar on the 100 Block of King Street.

Photo by Ross Stansfield

Soda fountain of Warfield's Drug Store on King and Pitt Streets. Photo taken in the 1920s.

Courtesy of Charles Sampson

Trudi Brookes, owner of the Green Connection plant store. The building is adjacent to Dockside Sales.

Photo by Ross Stansfield
Courtesy of ***Alexandria Port Packet***

The Fish Market was a warehouse for Lindsey Nicholson, but is now a restaurant. The Excalibur parked in front belongs to the fish market owner, Mr. Ray Giovannoni.

Photo by Ross Stansfield

501 Duke Street. This home was built by Dr. Peter Wise, physician and merchant. He mistakenly constructed it beyond the boundaries of the set-back line and it now extends onto the sidewalk. It has been owned by prominent individuals including Tobias Lear, Augustine Washington, and Mayor Simms, who owned it when the town surrendered to the British in 1814.

Photo by Ross Stansfield

View of Washington Street looking south around 1850. The old Cotton Factory, now an apartment building, is in the foreground. Castle Thunder is the large house on the perpendicular street.

Courtesy of Alexandria Library

Street cleaning around the turn of the century.
Courtesy of Charles Sampson

An old trolley on Royal Street in the early 1900s. Streetcar transportation began in Alexandria in the fall of 1892 when the Alexandria and Fairfax Passenger Railway Company added a new route within the city and changed its name to the Washington, Alexandria, and Mount Vernon Electric Railway. This line lasted a generation, transporting passengers from King Street along Fairfax to Franklin where it went west to Royal and then turned sharply south. Other tracks were added to this early route, including a run on King Street from Commonwealth to Royal. A powerhouse and carbarn were located east of the roadbed in New Alexandria south of Belle Haven Country Club. An end to the trolley came soon after Mr. R. L. May made the first bus run for the Columbia Pike Line in 1921. This led to the establishment of the Alexandria, Barcroft, and Washington Transit Company, Incorporated, in 1935. The A. B. & W. served Alexandria for many years before the coming of the modern Metro liners.

Courtesy of Seaport Inn

The corner water pumps, once an ordinary sight.

Courtesy of Mrs. Thomas Hulfish

"Uncle Jack" in Hume Springs area around
1900 with Mrs. Herbert Snowden in background.

Courtesy of Edith Snowden

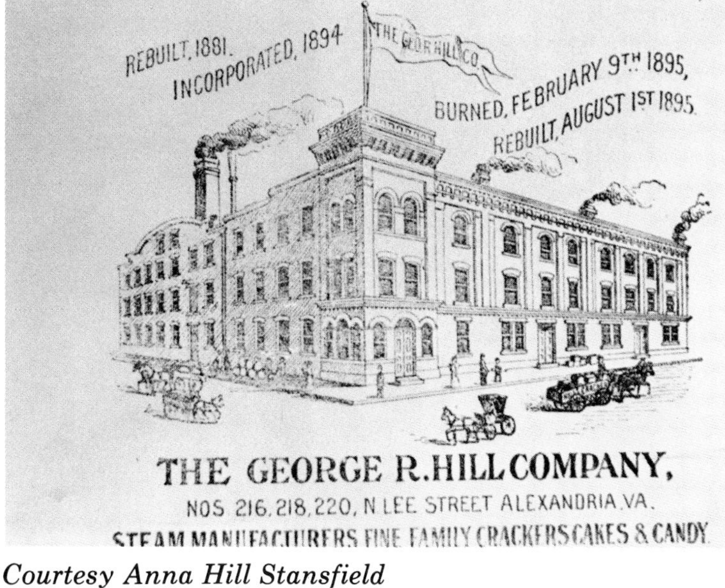

Courtesy Anna Hill Stansfield

Frank Michelbach's store on King Street around 1910.

Courtesy of Michelbach's Furniture

Hayman's in its second location on King Street in 1944. It is the oldest retail store owned by a single family. Inset shows Joseph Hayman, who opened the first store in 1902.

Courtesy of Ben Hayman

King Street in a snow storm in 1921.
Courtesy of Charles Sampson

Lower King Street under water. Seaport Inn and Dockside Sales are establishments in center building.

Courtesy of Charles Sampson

A flood in lower King Street in 1917.

Courtesy of Seaport Inn

Jones Point lighthouse in 1929.

Courtesy of National Archives

Carter Hall, 700 Block Prince Street, house of Daingerfield family in the 1880s. The Daingerfields gave most of the square—Prince to Columbus Streets—to Duke Street Hospital.

Courtesy of Alexandria Library

The Carlyle Apartments, photographed around 1929, no longer exist. The fashionable hotel was also known as Green Mansion and later the Braddock House. The Bank of Alexandria, the city's oldest, still stands as pictured here on the corner of North Fairfax and Cameron Streets.

Courtesy of Alexandria Library

Lindsey Nicholson Wholesale grocery was located on the southwest corner of King and Union Streets in 1929.

Courtesy of National Archives

The Duke Street Hospital, left, stood in the 700 block of Duke Street beside the John Daingerfield residence, right, at 221 South Washington Street. Both buildings have been razed. The hospital was the culmination of the work of Julia Johns, Daughter of Episcopal Bishop Johns of Virginia. Beginning as the Alexandria Infirmary Association in 1872, the hospital changed location several times before the construction of the Duke Street facility. The first unit was built in 1916 on property purchased from Edward L. Daingerfield. A west wing was added in 1934. The north and east wings were built in 1943 on land donated by the Daingerfield family. The Alexandria Hospital now operates from its Seminary Road location.

Courtesy of the Alexandria Library

The home of Dr. James Craik, 210 Duke Street, in 1929. A friend and personal physician of George Washington, as Surgeon-General of the Continental Army Craik often accompanied Washington into battle.

Courtesy of National Archives

The flounder house, like the fish, has one flat and sightless side. The flat side of this house on South Pitt Street can be seen to the left of the photo. Why were these curious houses built with their windowless walls? Some say it was the high tax on glass and expense of heating. Others claim it was due to the two year building stipulation placed on property owners. Doubtless these were contributing factors, but a final answer is left to one's imagination. In Europe the close proximity of homes makes buildings of this type not uncommon. Possibly homes were erected in anticipation of crowded quarters of the half acre lots. Or perhaps the new homeowners really did build half a house expecting to add the second portion on that rare day in the future that never came for so many of the "flounders." This is only one of the several flat-sided houses scattered over the city either standing alone or with additions disguising them as ordinary buildings.

Photo by Ross Stansfield

City Hall circa 1900.

Courtesy of Charles Sampson

The Loggia of the Jonah Thompson House,
209-211 North Fairfax Street.

Photo by Ross Stansfield

Popularly known as "The Lafayette House," this house at 301 South St. Asaph Street was the home of the Charles Calvert Smoot family for over eighty years. The name of Lafayette was given it when Mrs. Thomas Lawrason entertained the French general in 1824.

Photo by Paula Sussman

The Lyceum, 201 South Washington Street, a beautiful example of classical revival in American architecture. Founded in 1834 by Benjamin Hallowell, the structure housed The Library Company for many years. Recent documentation proves that its main foundation was built with bricks and stones from the old St. Mary's Chapel. The Lyceum now serves as the Bicentennial Center.

Courtesy of Alexandria Tourist Council

The Lyceum in 1940.

Courtesy of Alexandria Library

Children in the Smoot house (Lafayette House) in 1901. The colonial costumes were worn to celebrate Washington's birthday. Each child dressed as a favorite colonial individual.

Courtesy of Anna Hill Stansfield

Mrs. Charles Calvert Smoot, seated, at the wedding of Sybil Smoot and Edward Finley in 1911. The ceremony took place in the Smoot home.

Courtesy of Anna Hill Stansfield

Children in the Smoot's living room celebrating George Washington's birthday in 1932.

Courtesy of Anna Hill Stansfield

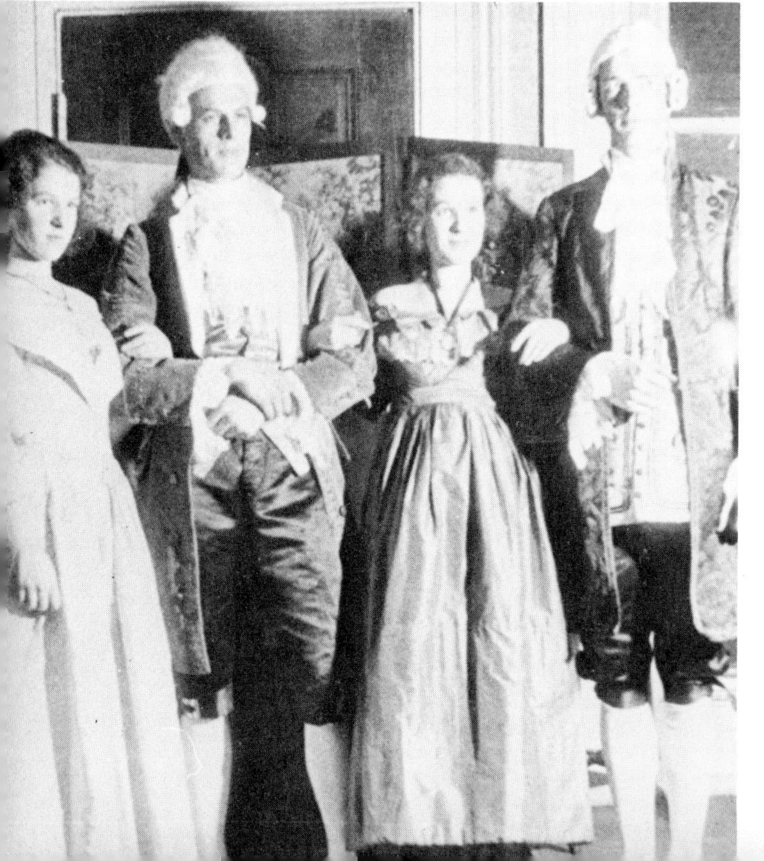

This elegant home has been known by the names "The Shadows," "The Hill House," or simply "617." Built in 1854 by Rueben Roberts, it was so far south on Washington Street that it was considered "out of town." Captain Samuel Bancroft Hussey bought the house in 1856 and came to it with his daughter, Melissa Ann, newly married to Robert Lewis Wood. A Northerner, she became enamored with the town and pledged her allegiance to the South during the Civil War. Her daughter, Ida Melissa Wood, married George Roberts Hill, thus the "Hill House" name.

Courtesy of Anna Hill Stansfield

The Hill twins with their brother and cousin, standing in the Hill House dining room before a Washington Birthnight Ball in 1932.

Courtesy of Anna Hill Stansfield

Verse of a poem written by Melissa Lovejoy Hill. The fence and house no longer exist.

"Three generations of us here and three
gone hence,
Have looked with pleasure on you, picket fence,
Familiar heritage;
But every fence and those it shelters must
Come down to dust,
And earth receive all like a ready host."

Courtesy of Anna Hill Stansfield

Headquarters, Hay Department Army of Potomac, July 1863.

Photo by Matthew Brady
Courtesy of National Archives

III. THE SOUL OF A CITY

A close look through the pages of history shows that the nineteenth century was not always kind to Alexandria. Yellow fever swept through the town in 1803 killing numerous residents. In 1832 illness and death again visited in the form of a cholera epidemic. Fire destroyed large numbers of buildings in 1810 and again in 1824. The city, once popular as a seaport, yielded first to larger ports and then to the success of the railroad. The monumental project of building a canal system ended in financial disaster. Twice the city was occupied by hostile forces, once in 1814 when the British held the city for five days, and then for the four long years of the Civil War.

In Alexandria's formative years it ranked above New York in importance as a trading center on the east coast. Tobacco and wheat were the primary export products, although the import-export business expanded greatly over time. As early as 1760 the first shipyards were established near Point Lumley on the south end of the waterfront. By 1762 Thomas Kirkpatrick had a ship under construction at West's Point. Soon many of the town's shops were equipped to outfit and supply seagoing vessels; at least eight ships were launched from Alexandria at the end of the eighteenth century. Shipping and shipbuilding were the lifeblood of the city.

The 1800s brought the decline and eventual end to the city's success in its maritime endeavors. Although the years preceding the War of 1812 saw twelve Alexandria-made vessels leave from the docks, British interference created severe problems for the port, and the shipbuilding industry was permanently damaged. Steam-powered ships took over trade from the sleek and romantic clipper ships, and the advantages of Alexandria as a seaport were gone by the start of the Civil War.

Local interest in shipbuilding did not revive until World War I. At that time Charles C. Carlin, Sr., helped develop the Virginia Shipbuilding Company at Franklin and Union Street Wharves (formerly Point Lumley). During this period nine steel ships constructed in Alexandria were launched. The end of daily use of Alexandria docks occurred in 1948 when the Norfolk and Washington Steamboat Company was liquidated. However, Alexandria did not lose all importance as a center for shipment of goods. The Potomac Yards, with 110 miles of railroad track, gave Alexandria national importance as a freight classifier. All north or southbound railway traffic was required to pass through the yards. During World War II the yards reached a peak of handling ten thousand cars in one day. The average had been five thousand. The Potomac Yards, owned by the Richmond, Fredericksburg, and Potomac Railroad Company, helped Alexandria remain a part of the shipping business on the east coast.

Other problems facing the city in the early 1800s involved finances and its incorporation within the Federal district. Alexandrians, taxed by the District of Columbia, realized few benefits. Real estate values climbed in Washington but dropped in Alexandria. By the mid-1820s the citizens were beginning to discuss retrocession. Early in 1846 a petition was sent to Congress, and in July that year their request was granted; Alexandria, District of Columbia, was returned to its home state of Virginia. Progress could be seen almost immediately. Virginia rescued the town from debts incurred by the canal project and set Alexandria back on its feet.

The advent of railroads further boosted the economy. The Orange and Alexandria, organized in 1849, was an important link to larger cities in the South. Two other routes were established in 1856, the Alexandria, Louden, and Hampshire Railway, and a connection to Washington. Citizens were optimistic during the productive decade preceding the Civil War, but by 1860 they could see storm clouds gathering.

Alexandria was the home town of the nation's first President. Loyalty to the country was strong, yet Alexandria was also a Southern city, and sentiments ran deep toward the Confederacy and all it held dear. By January 1861 the city was preparing for war. Families were forced to consider the possibility of leaving their homes as they observed the activity in Washington. A new militia company, The Old Dominion Rifles, was organized in early January with Captain Montgomery D. Corse and Lieutenant Arthur Herbert as leaders. By February this company joined with three others to form the Alexandria Battalion under the command of Corse, then a Major. On April 17, the Virginia Convention adopted an ordinance of secession, subject to referendum. Despite the fact it was not ratified until May 23, Robert E. Lee was appointed commander of the military and naval forces of Virginia on April 22. Two more militia companies were formed by the end of the month and a blockade placed on the Potomac by the Federal troops. On May 10 the telegraph wire between Alexandria and Washington was cut, and four days later Alexandrians found themselves facing the guns of the United States Sloop of War, the *Pawnee.*

It is easy to understand the state of unrest of the city when, on May 24, the famous Marshall House incident occurred. For several weeks the Confederate flag had been flying over King Street, and some Alexandrians claim that President Lincoln could see the flag and was disturbed by it. Whether or not this is true, the flag was a source of concern to another individual, Colonel Elmer E. Ellsworth. Ellsworth was Commander of the Eleventh New York Volunteers (also called the First New York Fire Zouaves). On May 24 three regiments crossed the Potomac to isolate and occupy Alexandria. Ellsworth's regiment landed at the foot of King Street at daybreak and proceeded into the city. Ellsworth stopped at the Marshall House and climbed three flights to tear down the flag. As he was returning to the street, James W. Jackson, the hotel proprietor, killed him with a shotgun blast. Witnessing the scene, Corporal Francis E. Brownell immediately killed Jackson. This incident, the first bloodshed in Northern Virginia, marked a period of despair that lasted for the four years of occupation.

As Union troops entered the city, the Sixth Alexandria Battalion quickly assembled and marched to the train depot, where it left for Manassas Junction. The Sixth Battalion was composed of the Alexandria militia companies and two cavalry companies from Fairfax County. One of the latter, Ball's Cavalry, was left behind and was captured by the Union soldiers. Some weeks later the Virginia volunteers became the Seventeenth Regiment of Virginia Volunteers with Colonel Corse as Commander.

Many families managed to leave their beloved city before Federal troops entered. Among those who left was the family of the Reverend John P. McGuire. McGuire's decision to leave was wise since the school of which he was principal, the Episcopal High School for Boys, was one of the many institutions taken over by Federal troops for hospital use. The Theological Seminary, Lyceum Hall, Baptist Church, and the First Presbyterian Church were also among the many buildings and homes that were used for this purpose. The county jail, Duke Street Slave Pen, Odd Fellows Hall, and Green's cabinet factory were converted to military prisons. The Mount Vernon Cotton Factory on Washington Street became a temporary shelter for prisoners en route to Northern camps.

From the journal of Robert L. Wood, May 26, 1861: "Our town is now under Martial Law. We have a regiment of Michigan men and one of the N.Y. Zouaves—The latter rather rough, but as far as I have heard respectful to the citizens. There was no resistance offered to them..."

From the journal of Melissa Ann Hussey, December 14, 1861: "You speak truly when you say Alexandria has been in a dream, but she has awakened to the sad realization of its purity being hourly polluted by the presence of Yankee men with their hired wives. Sooner would we have the cobwebs made by Southern spiders than encounter the hard faces and crude airs of the horde which has infested our town."

Alexandria was both a military base and an occupied city during the war. With few exceptions the military maintained the essential functions of the town. Alexandrians had little control over the operation of their city. The local newspaper, the *Gazette,* went underground. One of the incidents during this time was the burning of the *Gazette* office by the Union forces. The *Gazette* had printed an account of the capture of St. Paul's rector, the Reverend Kinsey John Stewart, who had omitted the prayer for the President of the United States from his service on February 2, 1862. In retaliation the *Gazette* office was ransacked and burned. The editor, Edgar Snowden, Jr., became one of several prisoners forced by the Union soldiers to ride military trains as hostage to prevent attacks from nearby Confederate soldiers. Another of these hostages was the Baptist minister, Dr. Bitting, who had openly spoken out against the Northern troops.

Citizens that remained Southern sympathizers were often harrassed or even imprisoned. John Woolfolk Burke of the Burke and Herbert Bank refused allegiance to the

Courtesy of Fort Belvoir Museum

On August 24, 1814, British-set blazes lit the skies above Washington. Three days later, Fort Washington, for six years a defense center on the Maryland shore, was blown up and abandoned by United States troops. As Captain James A. Gordon approached Alexandria with a force of seven vessels and two thousand men, members of the town council voted to surrender and to pay a ransom of one hundred thousand dollars, and on August 29 the town fell into enemy hands. No major incidnt occurred, although local tradesmen were forced to turn over merchandise and supplies the British captors needed. During the five day occupation plans for retaliation were put into effect. Fire ships were grouped at the Washington Navy Yard, and two gun batteries were formed on the Potomac. One was at Indian Head on the Maryland side. The other battery, commanded by Commodore David Porter, shown at left, was erected below Mount Vernon at the present site of Fort Belvoir. Commodore Porter's report of September 7, 1814, begins, "Agreeable to your order of the 31st I proceeded...to the white house on the West bank of the Potomac there to erect batteries and attempt the destruction of the Enemys Ships on their passage down the river."

For several days Porter's battery, with the aid of ships and land troops, tried to stop Gordon's down-river flight. Considerable damage was done during the battle, and Alexandria suffered two casualties, Robert Bowen and Robert Allison. Porter admired the Virginia men fighting with him. "The cool indifference of my Sailors to the danger to which they were exposed was very remarkable and the intrepidity of Captain Griffith of the Alexandria Artillery, his officers and men merit the highest eulogiums."

Gordon's fleet, with the confiscated goods, did manage to pass down the Potomac to the Chesapeake Bay. However, the city of Alexandria was left unharmed and Porter's battle on the Potomac will be remembered.

Alexandria Dragoons, 1810.

Courtesy of Robert Whitton

North and was for some time imprisoned in the District of Columbia. It was indeed a sad and difficult time for Alexandria.

In 1865 the city began a slow return to normalcy. By February hospitals were already being closed down and patients transferred to the Seminary. The Appomattox Treaty in April meant the return of families that had been refugees for the war years. In May the residents were again able to travel freely from Alexandria to Washington, official passes no longer a requirement. With the war over, Union soldiers gathered here one last time for a final review. Four years to the day after the occupation had begun, the Union troops received orders to leave the city. As rapidly as possible camps were disbanded and regiments left. July 7 ended the rule of the military governor. However, many months elapsed before all military control was relinquished in the southern city.

There are many consequences of war, some of which can be beneficial. Considering the objectives of this conflict that almost divided a great nation, it is important to realize how it affected the black population of Alexandria.

City records in 1784 list 543 slaves and fifty-two free blacks. By 1820 the number of slaves and free blacks was almost equal, 1,435 slaves and 1,168 free blacks. A free black had no rights under any law, but it is important to note that before the Civil War, Alexandria's colored population did not consist solely of slaves.

Toward the end of the war, many of the population of freed slaves were brought to Alexandria. Some settled along the outskirts of the city, others, needing medical care, were sent to a military hospital on Washington Street. In addition to this hospital two other facilities were opened for the newly freed Negroes, the L'Ouverture Hospital and Contraband Barracks.

Because the city was occupied by Union troops, Alexandria also became a haven for runaway slaves. The black population grew during the 1860s from 2,800 to more than seven thousand. This increase is reflected in the church history of that time.

Two churches served the black community before 1861, Alfred Street Baptist and Roberts Memorial Methodist. The Baptist congregation began meeting in private homes in 1803. Around 1818 the present building at 313 South Alfred Street was erected, although no Negro minister served until after 1863.

The congregation of Roberts Memorial (also Roberts Chapel) was originally affiliated with the Trinity Methodist Church. A group of

The John Marshall House, no longer standing, was built in 1850 on Wolfe Street. Named for a local merchant, the house served as a hospital for Union soldiers.

Photo by Matthew Brady
Courtesy of National Archives

Soldiers Rest, a convalescent camp for Union soldiers. Round-house is pictured left rear.

Courtesy of Southern Railway System

Union soldiers in front of the Old Dominion Bank on Prince and Lee Streets. This was the only bank able to repay all obligations to its depositors and creditors. This was due to the foresight and courage of William Henry Lambert, a cashier, who hid the money until it could be safely returned after the war.

Photo by Matthew Brady
Courtesy of National Archives

Provost Marshal's office at 515 King Street, used by a fire insurance company before occupation.

Photo by Matthew Brady
Courtesy of National Archives

four hundred colored members built a church on Washington Street in 1834. Originally called Davis Chapel for the Reverend Charles A. Davis, the name was dropped when Davis became a member of the Southern faction of the Methodist church following the split over the slavery issue. Bishop Robert Richford Roberts, now honored, was a pastor of Trinity Methodist Church in 1812. Roberts Memorial, like Alfred Street Baptist, did not have a black minister until after the Emancipation Proclamation of 1863.

Following the Proclamation came Beulah Baptist, the first of ten Baptist churches established to serve the expanding Negro community. Zion Baptist was built a year later, Third Baptist in 1865. Besides these, St. Joseph's Catholic Church was established by members of St. Mary's, and Meade Memorial was developed from Christ Church's congregation. Churches of other denominations have also taken their place in the community.

As blacks became property owners at the end of the nineteenth century, Negro neighborhoods developed throughout the city. "The Hill" and "May-Tie" referred to areas east of Washington Street in the south section. Far to the west were "Mudtown," "Seminary," and many names which have come and gone as neighborhoods have changed. However, the heritage and traditions remain part of the city's history. Family names of Seaton, Piper, Day, and Evans date back to Alexandria's earliest days. These are some of the families who have contributed to make Alexandria what it is today.

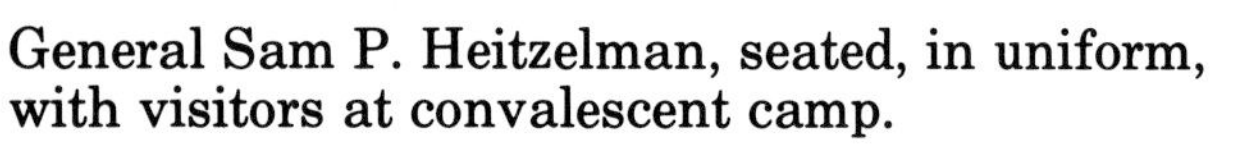

General Sam P. Heitzelman, seated, in uniform, with visitors at convalescent camp.

Photo by Matthew Brady
Courtesy of National Archives

Slave pen, 1318 Duke Street.

Courtesy of Alexandria Library

Stockade around machine shop and yard of Orange and Alexandria Railroad, erected by Brigadier General Herman Haupt in 1861 to guard trains from Confederate raiders.

Photo by Matthew Brady
Courtesy of National Archives

The slave prison.

Photo by Matthew Brady
Courtesy of National Archives

Federal troops at Alexandria station awaiting transportation to the battlefield. The engine is a captured Orange and Alexandria locomotive pressed into service on the United States Military Railroad.

Courtesy of Southern Railway System

HARPER'S WEEKLY.

A JOURNAL OF CIVILIZATION.

VOL. V.—NO. 233.] NEW YORK, SATURDAY, JUNE 15, 1861. [SINGLE COPIES SIX CENTS. $2 50 PER YEAR IN ADVANCE.

Publisher's Notice.

THE MURDER OF ELLSWORTH.

Courtesy of Robert G. Whitton

Track work along the Orange and Alexandria near Bull Run, probably in 1863. The locomotive was named for Brigadier Herman Haupt, chief of construction and rehabilitation for the United States Military Railway Service.

Courtesy of Southern Railway System

The infamous Marshall House.

Photo by Matthew Brady
Courtesy of National Archives

Precision Drill Team performs at Market Square for Marshall House rededication, May 1976.

Photo by Ross Stansfield
Courtesy of ***Alexandria Port Packet***

Civil War fort built in 1861 at the end of what is now Braddock Road in northwest Alexandria. It is named for Commander James Harmon Ward, first Union naval officer killed in conflict. The museum and officers' hut are reconstructions based on Matthew Brady photos.

Courtesy of Alexandria Tourist Council

Building in foreground (209 and 211 South St. Asaph) was confiscated by Union troops. Federal Judge John Underwood lived in 211 section of the home and General John P. Slough, responsible for defense of Washington and Northern Virginia, resided in 209. The center building is the old Post Office and across Prince Street is the Second Presbyterian Church, used as a hospital. Both have been razed.

Photo by Matthew Brady
Courtesy of Laurence Fawcett

First Virginia Regiment in front of the Carlyle House, April 1976.

Photo by Ross Stansfield

REG'T

Civil War reenactment at Fort Ward Park in June 1976.

Photos by Ross Stansfield
*Courtesy of **Alexandria Port Packet***

The Confederate soldier at the intersection of Washington and Prince Streets in a picture made before turn of the century.

Courtesy of Alexandria Library

GENERAL CORSE

Montgomery D. Corse was born in Alexandria in 1816. He served in the Mexican War as a Captain, after which he spent some time commanding a militia company in California. At the start of the Civil War he took command of the Seventeenth Regiment of Virginia Volunteers. He achieved the rank of Brigadier after Antietam and commanded a brigade in Pickett's Division in the Army of Northern Virginia. After Appomattox he became a prominent banker, served in the legislature, and was a force for reconciliation.

General Corse was chairman of the committee responsible for erecting the statue of the Confederate Veteran. He contributed his entire Mexican War pension and strived to ensure that the uniform and equipment were precisely correct. The statue is placed in the exact spot where the Seventeenth Virginia Regiment mustered and marched away to the battle of Bull Run.

General Montgomery D. Corse.

Courtesy of Rear Admiral A. C. Murdaugh

ALEXANDRIA CANAL

The biggest failure, both financially and practically, in Alexandria's history, was the building of the Alexandria Canal. The idea was originally conceived by George Washington in the hopes of establishing a route to the west. In 1785 the Potomac Company was formed with Washington as the president. Work began with a goal of joining the Potomac and Ohio Rivers. In 1828 the Potomac Company franchise was sold to the Chesapeake and Ohio Company on condition that the C & O Canal pass through Alexandria. To meet this stipulation the Alexandria Canal Company was chartered in 1830, and an aqueduct bridge was built across the Potomac at Georgetown. This insured that canal traffic would continue through Alexandria and not bypass the city by moving down the river. The expensive project was doomed, however, by the rapid development of railroads and steamships.

The canal was closed in 1887 at a tremendous loss for both public and private backers. The total cost of the project was one million, three hundred thousand dollars. It restricted the city's trade potential and financial capabilities for many years.

An aqueduct bridge on the canal system. The aqueduct at Georgetown was thirty feet wide and five feet deep. It was replaced by the Francis Scott Key Memorial in 1923.

Courtesy of National Archives

View of canal looking south from Georgetown to Alexandria.

Courtesy of National Archives

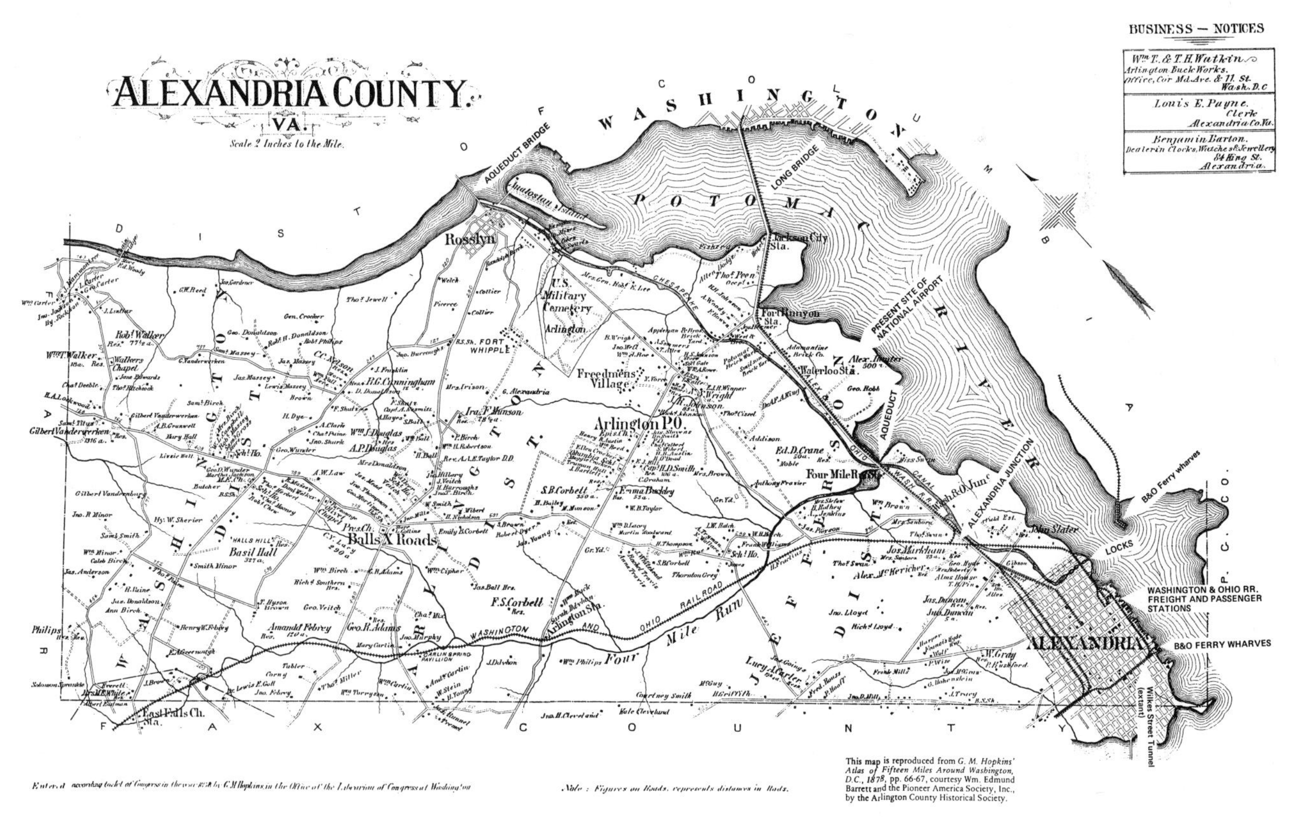

Map of Alexandria canal showing locks and aqueduct bridge.

Courtesy of Don Wells, Jr.

Fourth generation Alexandrian, Crystal Gray, great-granddaughter of John Strange, who was born 1879 on Wolfe Street. A railroad man, Mr. Strange has spent most of his life on Duke Street.

Photo by Elsa Rosenthal

Annie Withers Gray in 1911.

Courtesy of John Gray

Early 1900s, playing on the steps of an Alexandria home.

Courtesy of Mrs. Thomas Hulfish

Current photo of Mudtown. This street, Woods Place, honors one of the families that has resided in the community for generations. Only modern and attractive homes are present here today.

Photo by Ross Stansfield

FIRE FIGHTING

In Alexandria's early days every household had at least one leather bucket. This was not a convenience item but a fire-safety measure required by law. The size and number of buckets per household was determined by the number of able-bodied males and the dwelling size. Protection against fire was a serious concern. George Washington helped establish the first fire company, the Friendship Company, in 1774. While in Philadelphia in 1775 he purchased the city's first engine, a hand pumper which is on display today in the firehouse on South Alfred Street.

Being a member of a fire company was not only a grave responsibility but a prestigious job as well. By the end of the eighteenth century four fire companies were in operation. At the sound of alarm volunteers rushed to the firehouses. Often fierce competition ensued, particularly if the burning building displayed a fire mark showing it was insured. The first company at the scene had priority in fighting the fire and was appropriately rewarded. Citizens retained a strong loyalty to the company they joined. In addition to Friendship, the three companies prior to 1800 were the Sun (1775), the Relief Society (1788), and the Star (1799). Fire insurance was first offered by the Mutual Assurance Society established in 1799.

By 1838 three fire companies were added. The Crescent, located on King near Fayette Street, later merged with Friendship. The other two, both Hydraulions, were situated on Fairfax Street at Market Alley across from the Sun.

The town knew well the importance of fire protection as it had experienced severe fire damage twice before in 1810 and 1824. Later, in 1855, the citizens mourned the death of seven firemen who lost their lives in a fire on King Street. A monument was erected in Ivy Hill Cemetery as a tribute to these men and the bravery of all fire fighters.

During the occupation, Federal troops assumed the duties of fire fighting. They used the existing equipment but also maintained two horse-drawn steam engines. One of the engines was purchased by City Council in 1866, the same year an act passed for a paid department. The first salaried firemen were an engineer, Joseph Young, who received seventy dollars a month, and a driver and man to fire the boiler at forty dollars a month. A year later the former Relief Society reorganized as the Relief Hook and Ladder Company after purchase of the first hand-drawn ladder truck.

By 1906 the city owned three steam engines and had two volunteer fire companies as well as a hook and ladder company. Motorization occurred between 1919 and 1920. After annexation of the town of Potomac in 1930, Alexandria claimed four motorized companies. From 1947 to the present, four more companies have gone into service, the last added in June of the Bicentennial year.

Fire Department in 1919 when partially motorized.

Courtesy of Charles Sampson

Fire at Doniphan Building on King and Columbus Streets, January 2, 1929.

Courtesy of Charles Sampson

E. MILLER
CIGARS, CIGARETTES,
SOFT DRINKS, CANDIES

Fire at Kirk Brother's Grocery on King and Union, December 26, 1925.

Courtesy of Charles Sampson

Star Fire Company in 1867 at 116 South St. Asaph Street. The Relief Company's hand-drawn hook and ladder truck was temporarily stored here until it could be moved to the new firehouse on the 300 block of Prince Street.

Courtesy of Charles Sampson

Alexandria Fire Department football team in 1926.

Courtesy of Charles Sampson

The Columbia Number Four hand-drawn hose reel. The four wheeler stands in front of the firehouse in 1903, decorated for a parade.

Courtesy of Charles Sampson

Potomac Fire Company organized in 1924.
Courtesy of Charles Sampson

Fireman in uniform of a Hydraulion Company.
Courtesy of Charles Sampson

Joseph Young, Alexandria's first paid fireman.
Courtesy of Charles Sampson

The Smoot fire on May 12, 1909. The blaze at the Field mills and Smoot mills burned the entire 100 block of Cameron Street. The engine returning is Columbia Number Four steam engine.

Courtesy of Laurence Fawcett

Columbia fire engine Number Four was bought in 1871 in Philadelphia. This picture was taken in 1899 at 108 South St. Asaph Street.

Courtesy of Laurence Fawcett

Friendship Firehouse, now a museum at 107 South Alfred Street.

Courtesy of Alexandria Tourist Council

Monument erected in Ivy Hill Cemetery (King Street) honoring seven firemen who died fighting a blaze.

Photo by Ross Stansfield

Harvey Lunsford, left, on truck in 1920 with Ellis Cook, and being presented an award for fifty-eight years of service.

Courtesy of Charles Sampson

Photo by Ross Stansfield

POLICE DEPARTMENT

The Police Department in 1851 consisted of a nightwatchman appointed to patrol the streets of Alexandria from dusk to dawn. Sometime after the Civil War a system of "Nightwatch" and "Daywatch" was instituted. This system represented separate police departments, but was maintained until 1870 when a bill was introduced to consolidate the two sections. In the summer of 1870 a Captain, a Lieutenant, and twenty-one patrolmen were appointed and uniformed and became the first members of the Alexandria Police Department. The new department did not begin without problems, however. Its authority was immediately challenged by Mayor Hugh Latham, and Captain James F. Webster and Lieutenant John L. Smith found themselves in jail for disturbing the peace. Although the conflict lasted some time, the police department soon reached firm ground with Captain Webster serving as Chief for forty years.

During the last decades of the 1800s the police department primarily kept the city calm and clean. After World War I, its function became one of control and enforcement of traffic regulations and the Volstead Act. Upon repeal of the latter, traffic regulations and crime prevention were the main concerns.

The fifties saw many changes in the country which necessitated growth of the department. Salaries were increased, and women as well as men were added and new divisions organized. Under the leadership of Major Russell A. Hawes a K-9 Corps was started and the Police Cadet Program instituted. In 1970 a unique outdoor police pistol range was constructed and the newest program, the Police-Community Relations Unit, became effective.

Officer Watkins in uniform of the style worn around the 1890s.

Courtesy of Alexandria Police Department

The Alexandria Police Department in 1908. Seated are ex-Chief William F. Webster, Chief Good, and Lieutenants Smith and Pettis.

Courtesy of Hilda Pullman

Alexandria Traffic Squad, 1929.

Courtesy of Laura Southard

Entire compliment of Police Force in front of old Police Station in 1927. City Manager and members of City Council are in civilian clothes.

Courtesy of Laura Southard

Police baseball team at Baggett's Field (now the 1700 and 1800 block of King Street). Photo taken in the late 1920s.

Courtesy of Laura Southard

School crossing guards around 1965.
Courtesy of Alexandria Police Department

Motorcycle policeman with radar.
Courtesy of Alexandria Police Department

K. W. Smith at the corner of Commerce and Payne Streets. At a somewhat older age than pictured, Smith headed the Traffic Department, organizing it in 1937 and becoming director in 1944. Now retired, he has served on the Governor's Traffic Study Commission, the National Highway Safety Commission, and other committees. Photo taken around 1922.

Courtesy of Charles Sampson

Traffic Department headed by Chuck Kenyon, shown at left.

Photos by Ross Stansfield

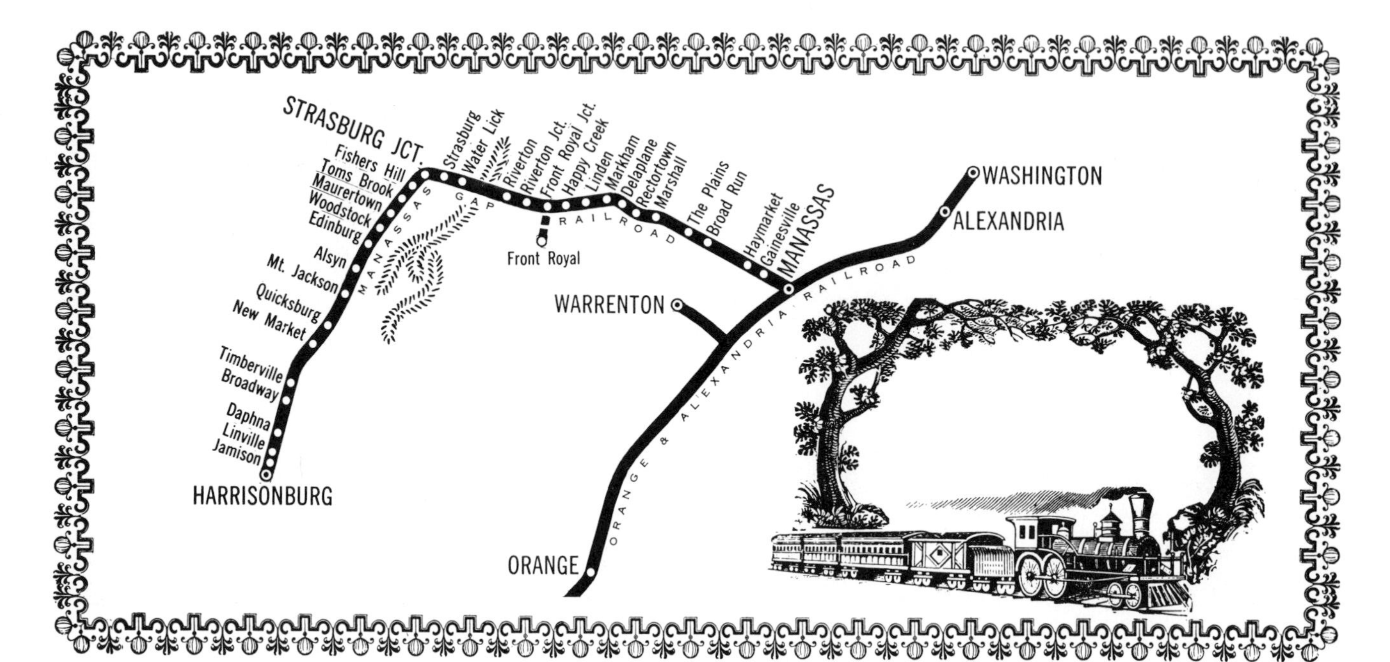

Courtesy of Southern Railway System

Southern Railway's Number 4501. The engineer takes a break in Front Royal before returning to Alexandria.

Photo by Ross Stansfield
Courtesy of ***Alexandria Port Packet***

Southern Railway's Number 630 on its special passenger trip between Alexandria and Charlottesville.

Photo by Ross Stansfield
*Courtesy of **Alexandria Port Packet***

In the cab of Southern Railway's Number 630.

Photo by Ross Stansfield
*Courtesy of **Alexandria Port Packet***

Southern Railway locomotive taken at Alexandria, Virginia, in 1940.

Courtesy of Southern Railway System

Train wreck on March 21, 1944, at Duke Street Bridge.

Courtesy of Frederick Tilp

Tearing up the railroad tracks on Wilkes Street.

Photo by Ross Stansfield

The railroad tunnel leading to the river on Wilkes Street after the tracks were taken up.

Photo by Ross Stansfield

No. 85 — 8 Station, 10/8 1872

To Orange, Alexandria & Manassas Railroad Co. Dr.

For Transporting the following articles from ______ to ______

	WEIGHT.	RATE.	AMOUNT.
1/2 Bbl Sugar 1/2 Do Syrup	385	14	54
1 Bbl Flour	200		20
1 Bbl	150	19	28
			$1.02
			60
Paid Charges.			
Total.			$1.62

Received Payment, E P Gaines, Freight Agent.

Freight bill of the Orange, Alexandria and Manassas Railroad Company, issued in 1872, after the Orange and Alexandria Railroad had merged with the Manassas Gap Railroad. This line is a predecessor line of Southern Railway.

Courtesy of Southern Railway System

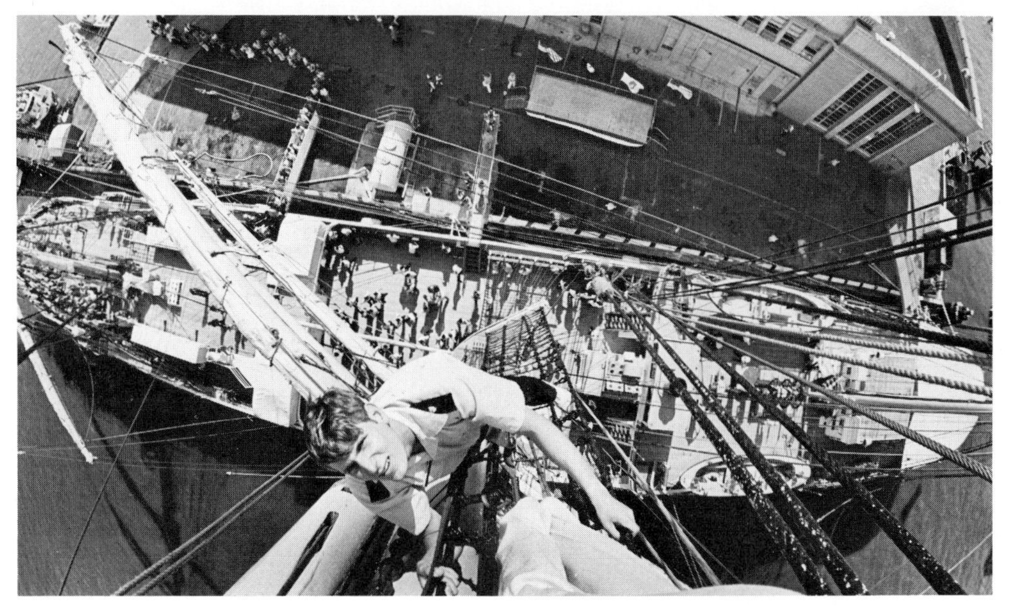

Looking down from the top of the *Eagle*, the Coast Guard Training Ship, when it docked in Alexandria.

Photo by James Oesch
Courtesy of ***Alexandria Gazette***

Virginia Shipbuilding Corporation in 1919.
Courtesy of Charles Sampson

The Coast Guard Training Ship, *Eagle,* one of sixteen square-riggers from around the world celebrating the Bicentennial.
Photo by Ross Stansfield

The *Eagle* passing by the Jones Point Lighthouse. This lighthouse, named for Cadwalder Jones, an Indian trader here in 1692, still sees activity although it is dwarfed by the Woodrow Wilson Bridge.

Photo by Ross Stansfield

Frank L. Wilkins and son in 1912. Wilkins was Jones Point Lighthouse keeper from 1907 to 1934.

Courtesy Frederick K. Tilp

Flagship *George Washington*, in 1852, painted by Bemenico Pavarro. The owner was Benjamin Higdon Lambert, who owned a fleet of sailing vessels that sank during the Civil War. This ship went around the world seven times. One of Lambert's sons saved the funds of the Old Dominion Bank during the occupation and another started the Listerine Company.

Courtesy of Mrs. Henry B. Allport

Ship loading grain at pier seven between Queen and Cameron Streets, May 1864.

Courtesy of Frederick Tilp

Alexandria Marine Railway and Shipbuilding Company in 1876.

Courtesy of Frederick Tilp

End of Prince Street at the strand in 1883.
Courtesy of Frederick Tilp

Old Dominion Boat Club at the base of King Street. It was started in 1890.

Photo by Ross Stansfield
Courtesy of ***Alexandria Port Packet***

The *William T. Hart*, launched on July 21, 1883. It was built by the J. P. Agnew and Company.

Courtesy of Frederick Tilp

On September 3, 1891, the *W. W. Corcoran* was beached at Notley Hall southeast across from Alexandria.

Courtesy of Frederick Tilp

W.W.CORCORA

Two views of docks between Duke and Prince Streets in 1912.

Courtesy of Frederick Tilp

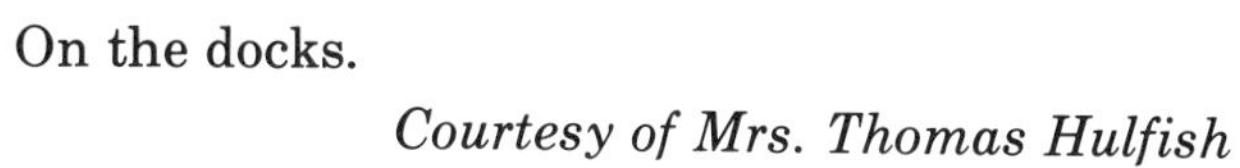

On the docks.

Courtesy of Mrs. Thomas Hulfish

Long boats on a Marine Railway, 1916. Agnew Shipbuilding Corporation.

Courtesy of Frederick Tilp

The *Charlotte Foster*, a Chesapeake Bay three sail bateau, hand built by Fred Davis, sailing on the Potomac. Photo taken in June 1976.

Photo by Ross Stansfield
Courtesy of ***Alexandria Port Packet***

The *USS Alexandria* on the Potomac in 1945. Launched on January 14, 1944, in Cleveland, the patrol frigate was christened in Alexandria and was sponsored by a member of the Daingerfield family.

Courtesy of National Archives

Agnew Shipbuilding Corporation at Battery Cove in 1920.

Courtesy of Frederick Tilp

INDUSTRY

Ford plant in 1932. The building is now owned by the government and used as a federal records center.

Courtesy of Frederick Tilp

A little known industry in Alexandria was the manufacturing of airplane parts. This factory at the foot of Duke Street had more than one owner. An unsuccessful attempt at airplane construction was made by a Mr. Richardson around 1914. Curtis Aircraft built planes around the time of World War I but outgrew this plant and moved to Maryland. Next came Henry Berliner, whose company built monoplanes for the United States Navy in the 1920s. Now occupying the site is Robinson Terminal Warehouse, a corporation storing newsprint.

Courtesy of Charles Sampson

Breaking ballast stones into gravel at the corner of Wilkes and south Alfred in 1908.

Courtesy of Frederick Tilp

The electric power plant for Alexandria (from the Wilson Line on the way to Mount Vernon).

Photo by Ross Stansfield

THEATER AND ART

A lively town, Alexandria never lacked amusements. Taverns provided space for musicians and actors to entertain enthusiastic audiences, and traveling thespians often stopped here. By 1797 plans were made to build a theater. The resulting Liberty Hall on Cameron Street was popular until it burned in 1871. Built around the late 1880s, Lannon's Opera House on the corner of King and Pitt Streets was the scene of plays and vaudeville acts for years.

After its establishment in 1934, Little Theater began the tradition of the revival play. Originally produced as a fund-raising project, the plays are authentic reproductions of dramatic works of Washington's time. "George" and "Martha" are always present, and guests are loudly announced upon arrival. When productions outgrew Gadsby's ballroom they moved outdoors to the coachyard. Meanwhile, Little Theater moved to a permanent location on the corner of Wilkes and St. Asaph Streets. Since 1961 the dramatic group has been staging performances there with "George" and "Martha" making their annual visits to view a current favorite of their day.

Art has recently flourished for a unique and interesting reason. In 1974 an art center opened in the huge building that was a torpedo factory for two wars and a Federal records center until 1970. A group of volunteers renovated and now maintain the former factory. Only the director and a janitor are needed as staff. For a nominal fee, the center rents space to individual artists, craftsmen, and a few art organizations. All work sold by the artists must be created at the center. Art work exhibited by the organizations is carefully judged and selected for display on the basis of artistic quality and not just salability. The project has proved to be beneficial to area artists and an asset to the community.

Before the Torpedo Factory project artists often displayed their work in "Fence Shows" sponsored by local businesses. In the 1950s the Junior League sponsored annual art fairs, and by 1958 the Alexandria School System began an Adult Art Education program under the direction of Joyce Field. With the formation of the Art Center, Alexandria now provides studios for the creative and a place for the art lover to wander and enjoy.

The Sharps and Flats photographed in 1900 in George H. Evans' yard at 320 South St. Asaph Street. Among those pictured are: Mrs. Louisa

Evans, Mrs. Raymond Hulfish, Mrs. Robert Downham, Mrs. Ellen Fawcett Cheeseman, Mr. Urban Lambert, and the organist-pianist of the group, Sherman B. Fowler, the mustachioed man in the back row on the left.

Courtesy of Ester Lambert

One of the Alexandria Little Theater productions of the 1975-1976 season was *70 Girls 70* as shown in this photo. The Little Theater on South St. Asaph and Wolfe Streets had produced such popular shows as *The Lion in Winter, Summer and Smoke,* and *Night of the Iguana.* The group gives six productions during a season plus the Revile play.

Photo by Ross Stansfield

Photo by Ross Stansfield
Courtesy of ***Alexandria Port Packet***

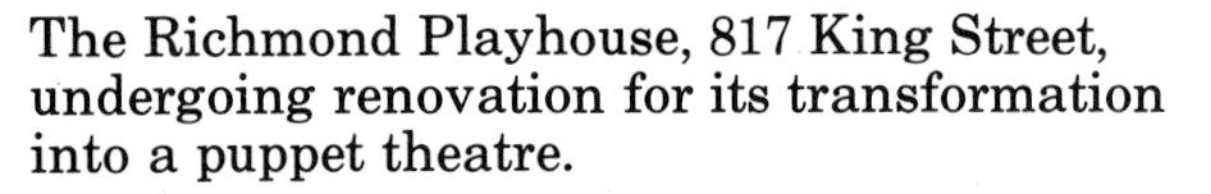

The Richmond Playhouse, 817 King Street, undergoing renovation for its transformation into a puppet theatre.

Photo by Ross Stansfield
Courtesy of ***Alexandria Port Packet***

A performance of *H. M. S. Pinafore* at the Old Opera House. Produced by the Sharps and Flats sometime before 1900.

Courtesy of Ester Lambert

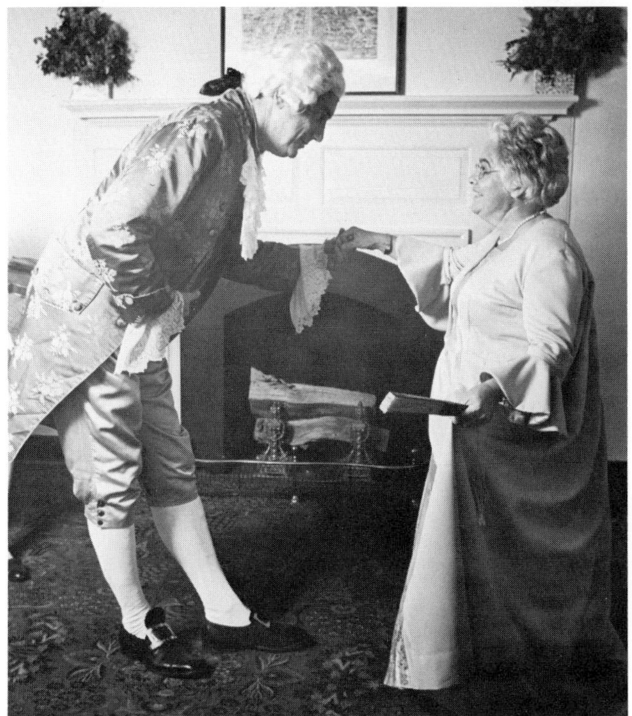

George and Martha represented by Charles T. Mulligan and Sally Brennan. Mr. and Mrs. Washington are always present for the Little Theater Revival Plays as well as other functions requiring the presence of the "President and First Lady."

Photo by Ross Stansfield

The Torpedo Factory as an art center in 1976.

Photo by Ross Stansfield

1943 aerial view of Torpedo Factory, now an art center.

Courtesy of National Archives

Brian McCall working on one of his etching plates at The Torpedo Factory.

Photo by Ross Stansfield

Dambalah Dolphus Smith, an artist at the Torpedo Factory.

Photo by Ross Stansfield

An Alexandria artist tries to capture the Il Porto Ristorante on the 100 Block of King Street.

Photo by Ross Stansfield

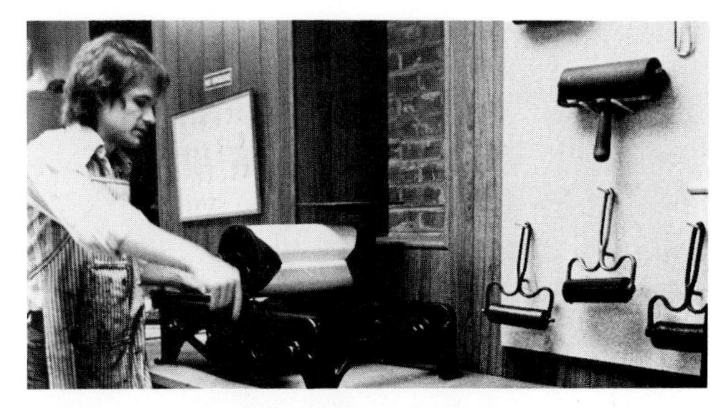

John Jacoby, printmaker and partner in The Engravers Press at 807 King Street.

Photo by Ross Stansfield

J. Damon Andrews has his studio in the Ann Lee home basement. He specializes in traditional studio lamp work style, producing handblown and handcrafted glassware.

Photo by Ross Stansfield

Ted Melpolder, painter, braving a rare winter snowstorm.

Photo by Ross Stansfield

Portrait artist Eve Myles at work at the Fort Ward Spring Craft Festival.

Photo by Ross Stansfield
Courtesy of ***Alexandria Port Packet***

Picture circa 1904 of Alexandria children in a production of the operetta *King Roughbeard*, with words and music written by Miss Melissa L. Hill and orchestrated and directed by Miss Dora Chinn, a music teacher at Arlington Institute.

Courtesy of Anna Hill Stansfield

OES players of the Martha Washington Chapter of Order of the Eastern Star. The group performed for several years during the twenties.

Courtesy of Ethel Stone

The *Son et Lumiere* show at Mount Vernon. This is a complex sound and light display given to us by the French Government for our Bicentennial.

Photo by Ross Stansfield
Courtesy of ***Alexandria Port Packet***

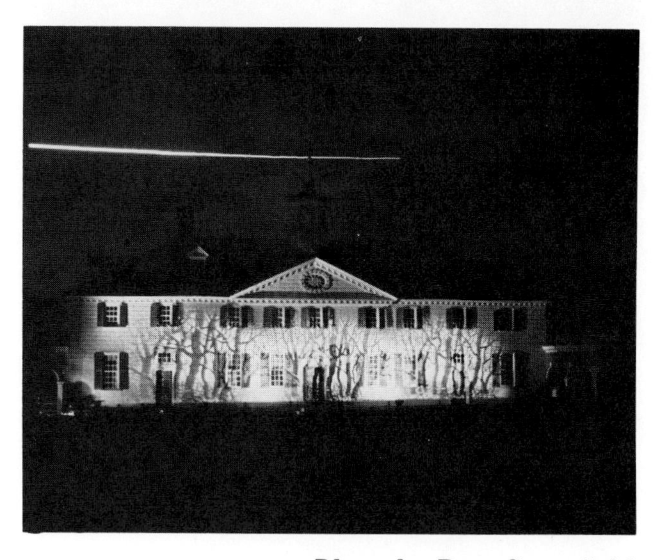

Photo by Ross Stansfield
Courtesy of ***Alexandria Port Packet***

FOLKLORE

No history is complete without the folklore and legends that are passed from generation to generation. Some stories are true, some are embellished incidents, others are beyond the realm of possibility but too enticing to overlook. Alexandrians know that in the last year of his life George Washington was so annoyed with the inefficiency of local firemen that he himself helped quell the blaze. But is it true that the ghost of Red Hill is the ship captain's wife? Who haunts the residential area on Russell Road where Braddock once marched and a Civil War hospital stood? Many know of the little girl whose quick retort quieted a Union soldier in front of St. Paul's Church, but what of the spirit of John Dundas that walked through Castle Thunder so many years ago? It is said that "Negro Tom" was an unschooled math genius and that President Jackson had his nose tweaked here.

What truth is there to these tales and myths? Fact may lie buried forever but the legends will remain an unforgettable part of the soul of this city.

The Female Stranger's secret lies silently in the grave in St. Paul's cemetery. She died in this room in Gadsby's Tavern in 1816. Who was she? Why was no one permitted to learn her identity? Has the truth ever been repeated to anyone who could unravel the mystery today?

Photo by Ross Stansfield

Courtesy of Frederick Tilp

This building at 515 North Washington Street, has been a cotton factory, the Portner Bottling Plant, a spark plug company (as pictured) and apartments. For fifteen years an unusual watchman has guarded the structure from the cupola. The watchman, shown in the insert, has not been on duty for some time. However, he still could return if desired—that is if no one has unstuffed his straw.

Courtesy of Dee K. Schwartz

The house at 210 Prince Street is often referred to as the Michael Swope House. A soldier in the Continental Army, Swope arrived in Alexandria in poor health. He moved into the Prince Street residence in 1784 with his wife and family and died in 1809 at age eighty-four. There are tales that the ghost that haunts the Swope House is the old soldier restlessly wandering the third floor. The present owner, however, claims not to believe in ghosts.

Photo by Ross Stansfield

View of King Street looking west from the Potomac. The Masonic Temple overlooks the city from Shooter's Hill. To the left is the Seaport Inn with the Old Dominion Boat Club in its waterfront spot on the right.

Photo by Ross Stansfield